COMPASSION IN DYING was able to acquire this book for you as a result of a grant from the Nicolov Foundation, whose generosity we gratefully acknowledge. We believe *Final Victory* is a powerful tool for patients and their caregivers alike, and are pleased to be able to provide it to you.

COMPASSION IN DYING provides national leadership to improve pain care and expand choice at the end of life, including the right to a dignified assisted death. COMPASSION offers support for the terminally ill, their caregivers and their physicians. Regardless of where you live, you have choices about your end of life care.

Phone: 503.221.9556 ❧ www.compassionindying.org

Final Victory

Taking Charge of the
Last Stages of Life

Final Victory

Facing Death on
Your Own Terms

THOMAS A. PRESTON, M.D.

FORUM
An Imprint of Prima Publishing

FORUM
An Imprint of Prima Publishing
3000 Lava Ridge Court
Roseville, CA 95661

PRIMA PUBLISHING, FORUM, and colophons are trademarks of Prima Communications Inc., registered with the United States Patent and Trademark Office.

Library of Congress Cataloging-in-Publication Data
Preston, Thomas A.
Final victory : taking charge of the last stages of life, facing death on your own terms / Thomas A. Preston.
p.   cm.
Includes index.
ISBN 0-7615-2899-7
1. Terminally ill.   2. Death.   3. Conduct of life.   I. Title.
R726.8.P73 2000
00-061869

00 01 02 HH 10 9 8 7 6 5 4 3 2 1
Printed in the United States of America

FORUM books are available at special discount for bulk purchases for educational, business, or sales promotion use.
For details, contact Special Sales
Prima Publishing
1-800-632-8676, ext. 4444

Visit us online at www.primaforum.com

To Tommy—

he taught us to laugh and to love and to live

CONTENTS

PREFACE

THE RELIEF OF unnecessary suffering is the purpose of this book. Since the time of my first clinical hospital experience, as a third-year medical student forty years ago, I have been constantly concerned, occasionally upset, and sometimes appalled when I've seen patients suffering. Prior to entering the profession of medicine, I had no illusion about the extent of suffering of the sick. Indeed, it was to do my fair share to alleviate suffering that I chose to forgo my training in electrical engineering and to work, in the language of the Hippocratic oath, "for the benefit of the sick."

The suffering of innocents has always been the major theme of human tragedy, and I cannot pretend to an understanding of it. But what we must struggle to see— with help—is the suffering forged of our own deeds. From the beginning of my medical career, I began to see within the sphere of suffering of the sick—occasionally—the handprints of physicians. Needless suffering may be basic to the human condition, but I was not prepared to accept excessive and preventable suffering that could be traced to the acts of physicians.

Most of the preventable suffering of patients under medical supervision is in those who are dying. To be sure, some non-dying patients suffer excessively because of insufficient treatment of pain or because of medical mistakes or complications of treatments. But physicians do best in applying their modern technological miracles to patients who will recover and who by definition have shorter, better-contained illnesses. Dying patients have three factors working against them. First, by the nature of having fatal diseases, dying patients have longer illnesses, attended by more severe periods of suffering. Second, although treatment initially gives most patients with terminal illnesses an extension of life with relatively good health, sooner or later medical treatment gives many the unintended by-product of increased suffering during slow and extended dying. Third, physicians are trained to cure patients, not to help them die, and the practice of medicine has not evolved to allow sufficient measures to counter the suffering that results from the new, prolonged ways of dying.

I am frequently asked, "What life event influenced you to write this book?" Journalists especially want to find the "human" story that explains why someone does what he does. The football player dedicates the game to his father who just died; the mother whose daughter dies in an automobile accident devotes her energy to combating the perils of drinking and driving. The physician who seeks means to peaceful dying must surely have watched a close relative die slowly, in agony.

I have no single dramatic life experience that incites me to action. My experience was simply of looking and hearing in emergency rooms, in clinic exam rooms, and in hospitals. Look behind the shields of modern dying and you can see patients pushed far beyond the natural limits of life, begging for release from the agony of the existence in which they are trapped.

Almost all of us have known someone who could not escape pain, debility, or degradation at the end of life. We have seen and heard the pleadings of dying patients but have been unable to move beyond the old patterns of passive acceptance of dying and deference to the traditions of physicians and medical practices. The tragedy of modern medicine is the inability of physicians to see their own hands in the inadvertent production of suffering, and the unwillingness of patients and their loved ones to counter this problem.

As always, the question is how best to solve the problem. In the world of technological innovation, every undesirable side effect triggers the search for a technological antidote. We develop technology to "treat" industrial air pollution. We treat allergic reactions to drugs with other drugs, and if a physician's heart catheter rips an artery, we operate to repair the damage. But what is the antidote for patients adrift in extended suffering after technology has run its useful course?

Our technology cannot turn back. It carries us forward, to newer, uncharted ways of dying. From ancient times we have had means to end life, but the full force of medical practice now pushes us relentlessly in the direction of prolonging life at all costs. For the dying patient in agony who pleads for release from life, dare we use our technology as an antidote to continued life?

The modern movement for physician-assisted suicide evolved from the search for a suitable antidote for suffering at the end of life. It is exceedingly important to keep in front of us this reason for advocacy of physician assistance in ending life. The goal is relief of suffering.

Although I was a plaintiff in the landmark assisted-suicide case of *Glucksberg* vs. *Washington* (State), my goal is not legalized assisted suicide—it is the relief of suffering of dying patients. If other means of relief of suffering are not available or effective, physician-assisted suicide may, under exceptional conditions, be a means for some to attain the goal.

When the U.S. Supreme Court in 1997 decided the *Glucksberg* vs. *Washington* case in conjunction with the companion case of *Quill* vs. *Vacco* (New York State), the Court upheld the states' laws, leaving physician-assisted suicide illegal in all states except Oregon, where state law allows it. But in their opinions the Supreme Court justices went to lengths to say that other legal means of relief of suffering, such as drug-induced continuous unconsciousness, were available, meaning that no patient need suffer excessively at the end of life. For example, Justice O'Connor wrote, "A patient who is suffering from a terminal illness and who is experiencing great pain has no legal barriers to obtaining medication, from qualified physicians, to alleviate that suffering, even to the point of causing unconsciousness and hastening death."[1]

In my opinion, the Supreme Court justices were incorrect to imply that dying patients generally do have access to effective means of relief of suffering—family and friends of innumerable patients who suffered greatly can attest to

---

1. Supreme Court of the United States, Nos. 96-110 and 95-1858, Justice O'Connor, concurring, p. 2.

the inability to obtain adequate relief. Nevertheless, the reasoning of the Supreme Court justices may be the defining event that led me to write this book, as it helped me to understand that since there is no legal barrier to effective relief of suffering, the solution is within our means. Our modern tragedy at the end of life requires a social, not technological, solution.

I offer this book to help dying patients attain relief of suffering by means for which there are no legal barriers. The barriers that still exist are in the minds of patients and physicians unable to break the traditional taboos of how we treat dying patients in an age of technological aggression. Physician-assisted suicide remains illegal in all states except Oregon, but it remains a desired option for many patients and is utilized by some. For this reason I include discussion of it as one of the means of obtaining peaceful dying. To the extent that patients and physicians are able to realize the Supreme Court's vision of legal means of alleviating suffering, physician-assisted suicide will become less necessary and less utilized. The future of dying is joint decision making by patient, family, and physician, with full use of modern medical methods to alleviate suffering while shortening the dying phase.

I am very far from the first to recognize the problem of excessive and unnecessary suffering of dying patients. I have seen for myself, but what I say I have learned from others. In the United States today there is a groundswell of change within the medical profession, aimed at reducing end-of-life suffering. The new direction is all to the good, but change from within the medical profession has never been easy, or rapid, and in our present culture we need a groundswell of patients and their loved ones asking for what the Supreme Court said is available. I hope this book will provide each reader with the means of helping to change our methods of dying so as to avoid unnecessary suffering and to attain more peaceful dying. The goal is attainable.

EPIGRAPH

HERODOTUS, THE FIRST historian, tells the story of Croesus, king of Lydia, who reigned from B.C. 560 to 546. Croesus conquered all of Asia Minor and was the most powerful ruler of the Greco-Persian area. Among the sages of Greece who came to visit and honor him was Solon, the Athenian lawmaker who had traveled throughout the known world. Croesus asked Solon, "Whom, of all the men that thou hast seen, dost thou deem the most happy?" Croesus asked because he considered himself to be the happiest of all mortals, rich and powerful as he was. But to his astonishment, Solon named an Athenian who, like Croesus, had lived a life of great comfort but who had died routing the enemy on the field of battle. The Athenian was the happiest, Solon explained, because "his end was surpassingly glorious."

When Croesus inquired who was next most happy, Solon told of two brothers who yoked themselves together to draw their mother a long distance by cart to a festival honoring the goddess Hera. In gratitude the mother besought Hera to bestow upon her sons the highest honor, which she did. After the holy banquet the two youths fell asleep in the temple and passed from the earth.

Croesus, dismayed that common men should be deemed happier, then asked Solon, "Why is my happiness so utterly set at naught by thee?" And Solon replied, "He who unites the greatest number of advantages, and then dies peaceably, that man alone, sire, is, in my judgment, entitled to bear the name of 'happy.' But in every matter it behooves us to mark well the end."

With this story Herodotus taught us that the happy person is the one who dies well.

ACKNOWLEDGMENTS

IT IS IMPOSSIBLE to acknowledge all those who have helped me in the development of this book, as the material is from uncountable sources within the extensive literature on medicine and related subjects. Indeed, my knowledge of the dying process and the many issues it presents does not exceed the sum of what I have learned from others—the many researchers, practicing physicians, mental health providers, and other health professionals, sociologists, medical and lay writers, ethicists, historians, lawyers (including the justices of the U.S. Supreme Court), and all who have contributed to the mass of reported information on the subject. So much for content. But for inspiration and human feeling, any acknowledgment would be empty without remembering the patients and their families who taught me the meaning of dying.

For offering helpful hints, suggestions, and corrections, I thank Tom Keller, Jinny Tesik, Jonathan Gavrin, M.D., Fred Marcus, M.D., Ronald Rubin, Patricia Weenolsen, and Barbara Nichols. I thank Robert Fulghum, who taught me not quite all I need to know about books and life's rituals, Hugh Straley, M.D., for exceptional help and direction, Phyllis Hatfield, who wielded extraordinary skill and judgment in emending "doctor-distant" language to common English, Assen Nicolov, for his passion in wanting to decrease the suffering of dying patients, and my agent, Arnold Goodman, ever gentle and persevering matchmaker, without whom you would not be reading this. I am indebted to Steve Martin, Andi Reese Brady, and Pat Henshaw at Prima Publishing and to Rosaleen Bertolino for their good sense, forbearance, and professionalism—and most of all for their kindness.

Authors always seem to acknowledge with gratitude the support of family in the undertaking of a book, but I never adequately understood the depth of understatement of this family role until I had traversed the process myself. Especially with the subject of this book, it took large doses of understanding and commitment, and the balance of frequent injections of humor, to tolerate discussion at the dinner table and beyond. To Molly, Stephanie, and Hilary I can only say thanks, and don't mention it.

PART ONE

Taking Charge from the Start

In this part, we'll discuss how to:

1. Prepare in advance. Prior planning is essential to having a peaceful death.

2. Understand how—in this age of medical technology— you are likely to die through unnatural medical extensions of the dying process.

3. Understand the ways by which physicians help patients die more peacefully.

4. Understand why you need a living will and durable power of attorney.

5. Be sure copies of your living will and durable power of attorney are in all of your medical files.

6. Discuss your plans with your family and friends to avoid misunderstandings about your wishes.

7. If you are family: Listen to, rather than advise, the person discussing her plans with you.

· 1 ·

Setting Your Course

SEVERAL YEARS AGO I met a patient, Margaret B., who had lived for almost two years in a long-term nursing care facility. Margaret was eighty-three years old and had been in excellent health until she developed chest pains. Her doctors sent her for diagnostic testing and then told her she needed open-heart surgery. She consented to the surgery, and the operation was technically a success. But then, three days after the operation, she had a stroke, and for a week it was touch-and-go as to whether she would recover consciousness. At the onset of the stroke, her breathing faltered, and it was necessary to use a mechanical ventilator (breathing machine) connected to a tube inserted into her windpipe. She did regain consciousness, but the stroke left her unable to speak or move one side of her body. Because she had pneumonia she had to stay connected to the ventilator for two months before she could breathe on her own. Then, because she gagged when she tried to swallow, the doctors operated to sew a feeding tube into her stomach. In this condition she was transferred to the nursing care facility. The doctors said there was "nothing more to do."

Almost two years later I had the opportunity to meet one of Margaret's daughters, who told me, while fighting back tears, that the entire family was unhappy and depressed over what had happened. She said they all wished Margaret had never had the operation and had been allowed to die after the stroke, which is what Margaret herself would have wanted. And now, her daughter, who felt responsible for what had happened, visited her mother every day and watched her sitting strapped into a wheelchair, drooling, unable to communicate, being kept alive with feedings through a stomach tube. I found the daughter's grief literally unbearable.

New Ways of Dying

IN THE OLD days we didn't give much thought to how we would die. Until about a hundred years ago the way people died was almost entirely a matter of fate. Death was said to be in the hands of God, or nature. Advance planning was limited to making sure our wills were in good order and finding someone to be guardian for our children in case we died.

Above all, dying was not a matter of human design, and no patient had any control over it. If there was nothing you could do about it, there was no reason to think much about it or to try to plan for it.

But times have changed, and yesterday's thinking no longer fits today's medical reality, which for most people means living longer and, often, dying more slowly, like

Margaret. In spite of its great technological gains, modern medicine has given us some very distressful new ways of dying. Most of us will face some form of high-tech dying, and we need to be ready for it. About three-quarters of Americans die in hospitals or medical facilities, where overly aggressive treatment is common; less than half who request "do not resuscitate" orders get them; a majority of dying patients experience severe, undertreated pain; and nearly 40 percent spend at least ten days in an intensive care unit before dying.

Knowing that it's highly likely that we could someday be in Margaret's tragic position, we need to explore the new medical realities and develop a new way of thinking so that we can deal with them. We need to learn how to make medical choices so that prolonging our life does not mean increasing our suffering, and we need to know how to minimize the suffering if it does happen. We need to understand why we can't wait until we are dying to plan for a better death.

There are countless stories like Margaret's—per haps you have personally witnessed such a tragedy of modern medicine. We can't blame these unhappy deaths entirely on doctors or the modern treatments and procedures they use, although they have a lot to do with what happens to us in the end. The bigger problem is combining the old way of thinking (that when and how we die is in the hands of "fate") with the new and sometimes miserable ways of passing on. As patients, if we just passively "allow" ourselves to go through all the possible life-extending procedures of modern medicine without using the equivalent modern means of going more peacefully, we run a large risk of dying with much suffering.

However, there are ways we can attain peaceful dying. We can use our doctors and their modern technology to plan and shape the way we die. We can avoid artificial extension of life when—as was the case with Margaret—it is a life of disability and suffering. We need to be able, when our time comes, to reduce or minimize our suffering, to be cared for without being a burden on our loved ones or leaving them with memories of our physical and emotional disintegration, to remain alert and in touch with our family and friends, to be spiritually ready to die, and to express our love while saying good-bye.

IF WE USE the old way of thinking about dying, we run a risk of dying badly. We need a new way of thinking to match the new, technology-driven ways of dying.

Being able to extend life and to control to some degree how we die is a truly revolutionary change, but we need to think about dying differently than we're used to in order to match the new health care that may prolong our life beyond a reasonable time. The new way of thinking means becoming involved ourselves in the medical management of our dying.

Preparing for Dying

TODAY, WE HAVE more control over our fate than we realize. We may not be able to plan our dying down to the last detail, but most of us can make a series of specific medical decisions, which, in general, will help to determine how we die. This is a revolutionary change from our old, fatalistic way of thinking about death and dying. Now most of us have the ability to set our own ground rules for the medical processes we will—and will not—go through.

At any time in your life, whether or not you are close to death, you can join with doctors and family members to make these important decisions. Within certain medical and legal limits, you have the opportunity to orchestrate how, and possibly when, you will die. A lot of people think, "Why should I bother planning how I die? What difference can it make—there's nothing I can do about it anyway."

Today, this sentiment is far from true. If you have a fatal disease, you can choose to do everything possible to slow the advance of the disease or cure it, or you can do nothing at all to delay the inevitability of death. You can choose to die in a hospital, a hospice facility, or a nursing home or at home. You can have nothing to alleviate your suffering, you can choose to be medicated even to unconsciousness at the end, or you can choose something in between. If you do not make these choices yourself, they will certainly be made for you—by physicians, other medical personnel, or your family—and you may not like the outcome.

The key to taking control of this decision-making process is preparation. This book is intended to help you to plan as well as possible for achieving your optimal way of dying.

Begin Planning While You're Still Healthy

WE ALL LIKE to think we aren't likely to die or become terminally ill until we are more than eighty-five years old. We might concede that it could happen at age eighty, or perhaps even during our seventies. Statistically, we may be right, but a strong dose of denial keeps us from facing the possibility that we could die earlier in life. A lot of us put off making out ordinary wills because it just doesn't seem necessary. Besides, why focus on something so morbid?

If we think of dying at all, we like to think we'll go quickly. We place ourselves on the other side of a mythical statistical barrier that protects us from a lingering death.

"If I die before I'm seventy-five or eighty, it will be from an accident, maybe a head-on collision, or perhaps something sudden like a heart attack or stroke. Only elderly people die slowly," we say to ourselves. "I should draw up a will, but planning how I'll die? If I get cancer, I can get help when they tell me I'm terminal, when it counts. It doesn't matter what I say or do now; it will all change anyway."

Even If You're Young . . .

It may be comforting to think that death will be fast and easy for you, but you need to consider the very real possibility that dying will be a protracted process. It's unwise to wait until you "begin" to die to plan for the way you want to die. Consider this: Those who suffer permanent unconsciousness after automobile accidents are often young. And this: If you happen to become fatally ill at a relatively young age, you have many more years to linger than older people do. And this: Although, with the proper planning, you have the means to control how you die, you cannot predict when a near-fatal accident might occur or a serious illness might leave you lingering in a coma.

Modern treatments that so spectacularly save many of us and restore us to useful life also unfortunately have the potential of transforming a quick death into a slow one. For example, suppose you suddenly slump over unconscious with a heart attack and someone calls the medics, who arrive five minutes later. Now suppose the medics successfully resuscitate you, but you are brain-damaged and do not awaken; at the hospital they connect you to a mechanical respirator. It's happened: You are deeply involved with advanced medical care, and you are unable to make the decisions that will determine your fate.

DYING WON'T just happen the way we might prefer—it takes preparation to avoid bad dying or to achieve good dying.

Suppose you don't recover consciousness in four to five days and the outlook for your recovery is poor. What do you want the doctors to do? Do you want them to keep you alive or to let you die? If your heart and other organs keep going but you don't awaken after three weeks, or six months, or two years, what next? Although uncommon, this could happen to any of us. Our doctors and our family need to know what we would want them to do, but if we haven't prepared in advance we can't tell them.

You May Not Know You're Sick

Even those who do not die suddenly may not have the time necessary for adequate planning. Many patients are sick with a fatal illness many months or more than a year before they learn what is happening to them. A cancer may grow and spread slowly, causing few symptoms and only slow weight loss or an unexplained fatigue. Worse yet, someone's doctor and family might know the diagnosis but not tell the patient because "it would kill him to find out."

Bernard, a man in his late sixties, had been increasingly short of breath for more than a year when he went to his doctor complaining of dizzy spells. He told the doctor, "I didn't want to upset my wife by complaining." Tests showed a large tumor in his lungs that had also spread to his brain. Before treatment could begin, he had a large stroke and lost the ability to talk. He also lost the chance to plan for this outcome.

A delay in realizing that you have a terminal illness can mean loss of the ability to plan during the early stages, when planning is still possible. Most drawn-out terminal illnesses, like cancer, also carry with them an increased risk of a sudden complication such as a heart attack, stroke, or hemorrhage. That is, even with a fatal disease that is usually lingering, you could suddenly lapse into permanent unconsciousness.

Some patients with a fatal illness have gone through

major surgery or are on a form of life support such as an artificial ventilator before they know they are dying. These patients are already past the time when they can effectively plan how they will die.

If we wait until we realize we are dying, the course of our disease may be so advanced that it may be too late to make essential end-of-life decisions ourselves. And the decisions we don't make could cost us a peaceful death.

Lawyers and estate planners tell us the most important thing we can do for our family when planning for our eventual death is to make out an ordinary will. Most of us have heard stories about someone who died unexpectedly without having made out a will and the mess and financial loss the absence of a will meant to the surviving family members. We also should apply this common sense to planning how we want to be taken care of when we are dying. By not doing so we risk leaving confusion, emotional pain, and frustration as major bequests to our families.

You can do this type of planning without dwelling on the morbid subject of dying, but don't wait. The sooner you lay out your course for the way you want to die, or, more particularly perhaps, the ways you *don't* want to die, the better chance you'll have of getting your way.

Setting Your Course in Advance

IF YOU HAVE ever run a canoe through white-water rapids, you may be familiar with the saying "steering is for still water." A person of average ability and strength can steer a canoe on a calm lake, but things are different in a fast-moving river. Once your canoe is into the rapid water, building up speed alarmingly, you have very little chance to change course. When the water gets swift, even the strongest person cannot change the direction of a canoe enough to alter the course through the rapids. Usually the course of your canoe is set by your position just before you enter the actual rapids. A good canoeist "reads" the rapids from upstream, in the still water, and positions his canoe to take the course least likely to crash him into the rocks along the way. In the same way, you need to position yourself properly to run through the rapids of dying.

As you approach the treacherous rapids of the end of life, you know you will die in the end, but you'd like the ride through the rapids to be as gentle as possible, not just for yourself but also for your family and friends. You want to avoid as much as possible the damage and hurt, to you and others, of the ragged rocks that line the rapids carrying you to the end. Once you're in those rapids you might find there is little you can do to change course. Positioning your boat properly in the still water above the rapids of dying, planning ahead, is your best chance of getting to the end peacefully. The remainder of this book tells you how to do this.

Summary

1. Planning in advance is the best way of getting to the end peacefully. The sooner you lay out your course for the way you want to die, or, more particularly perhaps, the ways

you *don't* want to die, the better chance you'll have of getting your way.

2. With the modern technologically based methods of dying in hospitals, if we just let dying "happen" we run a large risk of dying badly, or with much suffering. It takes preparation to avoid bad dying or to achieve good dying.

3. We need a new way of thinking about dying, which means becoming involved in the medical management of our dying.

4. Within limits we may direct where, when, and how we die by making decisions about how to use modern medical technology.

5. If you wait until you realize you are dying, the course of your disease may be so advanced that you have no time to make decisions you could have made weeks or months earlier. The time to begin preparations for dying is now, before getting sick with a fatal illness or suffering a potentially fatal accident.

· 2 ·

Medically Managed Dying

About 2,500 years ago the Greek philosopher Heraclitus contended that one cannot step into the same river twice. Rivers change in time, as do those who step into them. Reality, he was telling us, is not a thing, but a process. The way we die is also a process, changing with time and circumstances. If we are to understand how we get to the very end, the last minutes of life, we must understand the entire process of dying, including the meaning of medical acts during and at the end of the process of dying. In this way we can begin to properly set our course.

Under the old way of thinking, death just "happened." Many persons may still think of most deaths today as "natural," not understanding that medical technology has changed the processes of dying.

Dying is not an isolated act at the very end of life. In a biological sense, all of life is avoidance of dying. If we avoid dying from whooping cough at age five we then will die of some other cause at a later date. The more we can avoid the old, "natural," causes of death, the longer we live. Most of us who live to old age do so because we have protection from the elements and wild animals, our waste goes to landfills and sewage treatment plants, our water comes from purification stations, we wear seat belts, and toxins are eliminated from the air we breathe and the food we eat. The technology of public health helps us to avoid dying from industrial pollution, asbestosis, or lead poisoning, and, most important, it gets us past the scourge of infectious diseases. We no longer die of cholera, the plague, or polio. Rather, we live long enough to succumb to heart disease, stroke, and cancer.

Today we are living long enough to die in newer ways. The new ways of dying, of course, are the result of man-made, technologically driven changes, not natural changes. Although we consider it a natural death when someone dies of a stroke at the age of seventy-nine, this person most likely would have died earlier of some quite different cause had it not been for the myriad technologies of public health. Modern technology unnaturally and quietly alters the processes of our dying, and for most of us this means dying later in life in different, unnatural ways.

Changing Our Dying Processes

BACK IN THE time of Hippocrates, physicians did not wish to be associated with fatal outcomes and preferred to back away from treating the dying if they could do nothing to prolong life. In time, physicians came to attend at deathbeds, though they had little to offer beyond holding the hand of the dying person as the family looked on.

The process of dying changed dramatically with the

advent of technological medicine in the middle of the twentieth century. Physicians were able to cure many patients who would otherwise have died and to extend the lives of most patients with fatal conditions.

Today, people are cured every day in hospitals and in doctors' offices. Treatments with medicines cure us of otherwise fatal infections and prevent fatal strokes and heart attacks. Operations save us from death by blocked bile ducts, tumors, bowel obstructions, and other fairly common conditions such as skin cancers that might have killed us if allowed to take their natural course. Patients die later in life of other illnesses, such as cancer or Alzheimer's disease, that may involve longer, more debilitating deaths.

The medical profession points with pride to the fact that most patients with incurable illnesses have their lives extended for days, weeks, months, or even years through medical intervention. Today, treatment invariably alters the natural process of dying. This is a fundamental, historic change in the way patients die and in the involvement of physicians in the management of dying.

Treatment Changes How We Die

The man with lung cancer now survives the first bout of pneumonia caused by his cancer that most likely would have caused his death a few short years ago. He lives on for a year or more with the help of antibiotics, chemotherapy, and surgery until the spreading cancer leaves him so debilitated that he must be connected to a mechanical respirator in order to stay alive. The woman with heart failure stays alive with medicines and a pacemaker but is dying slowly because her weak heart cannot supply her kidneys, liver, and intestines with enough blood to function. A patient who has surgery for throat cancer dies years later of infections secondary to side effects of the medicines he must take to prevent recurrence of the cancer.

Nowadays, older-age illnesses are more prolonged and carry longer periods of debility and suffering. This leads to more medical interventions and treatments, involving more decisions as to how to use the medical technology available. With the exceptions of those who die suddenly and those who cannot or do not get medical care, virtually every patient with a fatal illness has some technological prolongation of life beyond natural dying, whether it be by a dramatic treatment such as an organ transplant or a simple treatment like a water pill (diuretic) or an antibiotic.

MODERN MEDICINE changes our dying processes directly by curing us of many previously fatal illnesses and by extending the lives of most people who have fatal conditions.

For most patients, their extended life is ultimately at the price of deteriorating organs, increasing debility, and a different and sometimes more severe set of symptoms and medical problems at the end. Most patients now die in conditions unknown just fifty years ago. The final rapids we must run in our process of dying are now far different, usually much longer, and sometimes much more treacherous than the ones our ancestors had to navigate.

Dying Unnaturally

THESE DAYS, ABOUT 80 percent of Americans die in medical facilities, most at a time and in a way determined by medical interventions and the physicians who control them (see table 1). Physicians help patients extend life for as long as technologically possible. But the unanticipated results of technological life extension are new, unnatural conditions of extended dying—conditions that Hippocrates never imagined: Patients connected to artificial ventilators for weeks or months on end, transplanted organs, continuous intravenous infusions of drugs or blood products, heart-assist pumps, kidney dialysis, and sometimes two or more of these or other medical technologies at the same time.

Many people have come to realize that the new modes of dying are not always preferable to the old. Pneumonia used to be called "the old man's friend" because it brought death painlessly and swiftly. But now pneumonia is easy to treat, and the old man must live to die later, often more slowly and with extended disability and suffering. For example, Horace, an eighty-seven-year-old man with lung cancer, was dying of pneumonia, but his doctors "saved" him with antibiotics. However, the damage to his lungs was so extensive he could then only survive hooked up to an artificial ventilator. He lived this way for another four weeks, when he went slowly into shock and died.

Patients and their families began to rebel against medical extension of life when it resulted in processes of dying devoid of meaning and with prolonged suffering. Faced with this problem, physicians had to find new medical methods to help their patients end the excessive suffering of unnatural dying, or at least not extend it needlessly. When a patient has a complication from a treatment—such as an infection after an operation—the physician uses another treatment to counter the complication. Similarly, when modern treatments produced the unforeseen complication of prolonged and difficult dying, physicians needed new methods to counter or at least limit the complication.

Although many people still think of "natural" dying as best, we have done everything in our power to prevent natural dying in order to prolong life. As physicians

---

TABLE 1
Modern Methods of Medically Managed Dying

1. Non-resuscitation
2. Discontinuation of life-support therapy including
   - artificial ventilator
   - feeding tube or intravenous nourishment
   - essential drugs
   - kidney dialysis
   - pacemaker or heart defibrillator
3. Aggressive comfort care
   - morphine drip
4. Terminal sedation

---

gradually developed—and the public accepted—unnatural, technological means of extending life, there was no going back to the old, truly natural, ways of dying. As we prolong life, each complication and the necessary antidotes take us further into new and unnatural territory. These new technologies have brought with them new language necessary both to explain and justify the interventions.

Non-Resuscitation

ONE OF THE most dramatic means of extending life, resuscitation of a patient by an electrical shock to the heart, became widely available in the 1960s. Most people had no trouble accepting this technological advance because the gain seemed so immediate and obvious. The cause of sudden, unexpected natural death is most commonly a malfunctioning of the heart's electrical system, a condition called *ventricular fibrillation* (another type, atrial fibrillation, is not fatal and is usually easily controlled and compatible with long life). Many patients who get ventricular fibrillation, which is otherwise quickly fatal, have a quirky disarrangement that, once corrected, might not occur again for years. Some people get the problem while under anesthesia for a routine operation, while having a heart attack from which they could otherwise recover, or because of side effects of drugs.

In many of these cases defibrillation with an electrical shock corrects the situation, and the patients recover and resume normal or near-normal lives. Others may remain sick but gain months of extra life.

Pitfalls of Resuscitation

However, even patients who have been shocked out of a fatal heart condition and resume normal living will never die "naturally" in the sense of dying the way nature would have done it because of the artificial electrical resuscitation. Since they did not die naturally from the ventricular fibrillation, they must die later, in some other way. This raises a potentially serious problem. Some patients who are resuscitated may not resume normal lives and, moreover, may be brought back to unnatural conditions of extended suffering.

About twenty years ago I helped care for Bill, a patient who at age eighty-six had had three heart attacks, was too weak to sit up in bed, and was hospitalized because of severe breathlessness. We had tried everything and had no further means of making his heart better. On the day after he entered the hospital his heart fibrillated; if the condition had been left uncorrected he would have died, but the house staff used electrical shock to restore his scarred heart to regular beating. His medicines were increased, but the same thing with the same response happened again that evening. By then he was almost too weak to

THERE'S NOTHING natural about the way we die these days. Physicians have had to find new medical methods to help patients end the excessive suffering of unnatural dying.

talk, and with our most powerful medicines we could not keep his blood pressure at acceptable levels. I informally suggested to the house staff that he not be resuscitated again because it would only prolong his suffering, but for a third time his heart fibrillated, and again he was shocked back to consciousness. When I heard of the incident I ran to see him, and he asked, "Why have you done this to me? Why will you not let me die?"

When I asked the same of the intern and resident who last resuscitated him, they replied, "Because it would be the same as killing not to do everything possible to keep a patient alive." These young doctors were unable to refrain from resuscitation, the medical procedure they knew and could perform so well. Since resuscitation was something doctors could "do" for every patient whose heart stopped, it had become standard medical practice to use the procedure whenever possible. It would take an additional mechanism, an act of forbearance, to prevent the standard act of resuscitation.

Overuse of Resuscitation

The doctors who kept resuscitating the eighty-six-year-old man refused to use the new medical practice of "do not resuscitate," which means deciding in advance to not resuscitate if the heart fibrillates or stops. For these doctors, the issue was not the condition and wish of the patient, but how they viewed the manner in which they would let him die. The morality of resuscitating or not resuscitating, as perceived by these young physicians, had nothing to do with what was best for the patient and everything to do with how they thought their professional colleagues and other observers would view their specific medical act. This is an important lesson for us—as potential dying patients—because it demonstrates how difficult it is for physicians to not use an otherwise useful technology at times when it is not of benefit and may even harm patients by keeping them alive.

When resuscitation became widely available and physicians learned how to do it, they did it whenever possible. It could be done almost endlessly, applied to virtually everyone for whatever reason, and sometimes physicians even did it to a patient ten or more times after it became clear that the patient would only start to die again soon after each resuscitation.

The ability to endlessly resuscitate became a harmful side effect or complication of a new technology. Physicians had to find a way of foregoing this treatment when it was inappropriate or likely to increase suffering. They had to work out the whens and wheres of "do not resuscitate." But this was not easy for some physicians and laypersons, who felt that not to resuscitate amounted to "killing" the patient.

The key to society's eventual acceptance of non-resuscitation in certain cases lay in understanding that further treatment would only add to a patient's misery. Implicit in that understanding was the knowledge that, prior to letting a patient die, physicians had done everything reasonable and the patient's life had actually been extended beyond its natural course. At the same time patients were gaining the legal right to refuse any medical treatment. If a patient asked in advance not to be resuscitated, doctors could honor the request without appearing to be "killing" by denying life-saving treatment. Non-resuscitation then came to be called "forgoing undesirable treatment" and "allowing the patient to die naturally."

Because society was able to change its language, shifting the focus from the act (or the withholding of an act) to the underlying disease, physicians became directly involved in how and when their patients died. Until the acceptance of non-resuscitation, physicians had changed the process of dying through "positive" interventions intended to prolong life (although in most instances it was not possible to say how long an antibiotic or operation prolonged a patient's life). Now physicians were making decisions intended not to prolong life but to allow it to end. This marked the beginning of troubled ethical waters, because although almost no one has an ethical problem with saving lives, many people believe that only God can make decisions that lead to ending life. This fundamental belief underlies past, present, and presumably future de-bates over the appropriateness of medical management of dying.

The Language of Non-Resuscitation

Many say the language of "foregoing undesirable treatment" and "allowing the patient to die naturally" is a fiction that hides physicians' involvement in helping patients die. Regardless of its appropriateness or correctness, the language that physicians, lawyers, and medical ethicists developed to describe non-resuscitation allowed doctors to begin playing a more direct role in helping patients die.

This small step in planning for how a patient might die marked the beginning of the revolution in managing the process of dying through active patient participation, although it took a while for physicians to "allow" patients to participate in this decision.

Withdrawing Life-Sustaining Therapy

OTHER MEANS OF helping patients die soon followed. With the consent of patients, or patients' guardians, physicians can now discontinue life-support therapy for patients terminally ill with no chance for recovery. Death then ensues. Most people have heard of "pulling the plug" on a patient, which is perhaps the most dramatic means of withdrawing life-sustaining therapy and refers to disconnecting the ventilator on which a dying patient is dependent. After the ventilator has been disconnected, the patient soon dies of asphyxiation. However, because patients fight to breathe after being disconnected from a ventilator and the distress of slow asphyxiation can be great, it is common practice to sedate the patient into unconsciousness before disconnecting the ventilator, so that the patient has no feel-ing of choking. Even so, reflexes may make unconscious patients continue to struggle to breathe after disconnection from the ventilator. Although physicians believe patients who are sedated have no sensation, they cannot be absolutely sure a struggling patient has no distress. Therefore, and since the patient is dying, in order to prevent this physical struggle, physicians sometimes administer a medicine that paralyzes the muscles of breathing so the patient quickly dies.

Physician Participation in "Allowing to Die"

Notice, however, the very active involvement required of doctors and nurses to "allow" this sort of dying. When this practice began about twenty-five years ago, many said it was "killing," and there was vigorous opposition to the practice within the medical profession and by many others who considered it unethical. It took time and several celebrated court cases to establish the legal right to honor the request of a patient or the patient's agent to disconnect a ventilator when that act would in all probability lead to the death of the patient.

PROFESSIONAL and social beliefs can make physicians keep using medical technologies even when they are inappropriate.

Karen Anne Quinlan was twenty-one years old when she collapsed at a party. She was treated but remained in a persistent vegetative (unresponsive) state and existed on an artificial respirator with nourishment through a stomach tube. Five months after the accident, when it was clear Karen would not recover, her father requested that the respirator be removed. Her physicians refused the request. The case went to the New Jersey Supreme Court, where a spokesman for the Catholic Church supported the father's request. The court ruled in favor of the right of an individual or surrogate for the patient to refuse treatment—even if it meant probable death.

Physicians and medical ethicists now describe the practice of withdrawing life-sustaining treatment as "allowing the patient to die naturally," although there is absolutely nothing natural about this method of dying. It is an unnatural means of ending an unnatural prolongation of life.

Other Means of "Allowing to Die"

The right of a patient to discontinue life-sustaining treatment is now firmly established, legally and medically. Other means of withdrawal or discontinuation of life-sustaining treatments include removing or not using a feeding tube inserted into a patient's stomach, stopping intravenous feedings, stopping kidney dialysis, and stopping certain drugs necessary to sustain life in some patients. Physicians allow some patients to die by turning off their implanted heart defibrillator or pacemaker (although most pacemakers cannot be turned off entirely). All these methods of withdrawing treatment result in patients' dying. We say that by so doing we allow patients to "die naturally," but of course there's nothing natural about these new processes of dying. Hippocrates never had a patient kept alive for weeks, months, or even years by a ventilator, or by feedings through a stomach tube. Patients who die by discontinuation of life-sustaining treatment are doing so in the new manner of medical management of dying.

Aggressive Comfort Care

MORE AND MORE patients today are enduring conditions of extended dying, and for some of them reaching the end of life seems to be the only means of ending their suffering. For those who beg to die but who have no life-sustaining treatment to stop, the only medical means of ending life is to administer a drug specifically for that purpose. However, when we focus only on the specific life-ending act, we run afoul of cultural or religious prohibitions against "killing," not to mention the law in most states.

Physicians have a conflict when a dying patient is suffering; the medical standard is to sustain life as long as possible. A doctor cannot easily and abruptly shift professional gears from prolonging a patient's life to deliberately helping to end it. One solution is to use routine medical practices, which in their usual applications are not known to cause death but which may ease the path to death without being the primary instrument of it.

The most common professional practice for helping to end life peacefully is the use of "aggressive comfort care," by which is meant the use of painkillers, sedatives, or other drugs or techniques to abolish pain or other uncomfortable symptoms. In medical circles this is also known as *palliative* care. When physicians or medical writers use the term "aggressive" to describe comfort, or palliative, care, in general they mean using enough drugs to abolish the patient's symptoms entirely or nearly so, even at the risk of the side effect of sedation or unconsciousness. We will discuss aggressive comfort care more extensively in later chapters and for now will consider only the most extreme forms available to physicians for use in helping patients die peacefully.

Morphine

The aggressive use of morphine or similar drugs to abolish pain or other symptoms is the most common medical technique for easing the path to death without being the primary instrument of it. A continuous intravenous infusion of morphine can abolish pain in about 90 to 95 percent of terminally ill patients, although the dose required for pain control may in some cases render the patient nearly unconscious. In fact, morphine given in excessively high doses can stop breathing, and so treatment with high-dose morphine carries the risk of ending life, although it rarely does so. Also, it is possible that some patients at death's doorstep may literally be kept alive by the stimulant effect of pain, and elimination of that stimulus may "allow" the patient to die earlier than would have happened without the morphine.

> **PROBABLY THE** most common medical technique for easing the path to death without being the primary instrument of it is the aggressive use of morphine or similar drugs.

Under what is known as "the principle of the double effect" (accepted by the law, the medical profession, and virtually all religious groups), it is allowable for a physician to give a drug such as morphine to a dying patient for the purpose of relieving suffering even though it may have a second, "foreseen but unintended, consequence"—death. If a patient at the end of life has pain or discomfort so severe that it can be controlled only with doses of morphine so high the patient becomes unconscious, a physician may, as a matter of good medical care, give such a high dose. It therefore happens sometimes that a physician administers a morphine drip for the purpose of pain control, with a gradual increase in the dose for complete control of suffering, until the patient slips into a coma and eventually dies.

Most patients who receive morphine drips at the end of life are suffering greatly and are nearly comatose. I remember well Louise, about seventy years old, who had suffered a series of heart attacks. Her heart was so weak she was severely short of breath and her blood pressure had dropped to "shock" levels. When the doctors had done everything possible, they stopped all other medicines and began the intravenous morphine. To the relief of the family she soon quieted, her breathing became more comfortable, and she died peacefully about twelve hours later.

For most patients who receive a morphine drip at the end of life, the drug relieves their pain and suffering but does not shorten their life. For those patients in whom the morphine induces a coma, this technique may shorten their life—but by hours or a few days at most. The reality is we really can't know for sure when they would have died had they not had the morphine. The aggressive use of morphine for dying patients is somewhat controversial because of the potential for physicians to give enough of it to intentionally hasten dying. How often this happens is quite unknown.

Regardless, the practice of a morphine drip to relieve or abolish suffering at end of life is legal in all states and is widely accepted and is practiced by most physicians at one time or another as a part of good comfort care for dying patients. In the larger picture of the medical management of how patients die, this is a very important method of controlling the time and way of dying.

Terminal Sedation

TERMINAL SEDATION IS a less commonly used medical intervention to relieve uncontrollable symptoms in a dying patient. When given intravenously in sedative doses, barbiturates or other drugs can render a patient unconscious without leading directly to death. By this means, physicians can induce ongoing unconsciousness to relieve symptoms, much the same as with a morphine drip but with better control and more effective sedation than is usually possible with morphine. If a patient is suffering so much as to require unconsciousness to relieve symptoms, there is no point in allowing a return of extreme pain with episodes of intermittent consciousness, as can happen with morphine. Therefore, terminal sedation continues until the patient dies.

Following the induction of sedation to unconsciousness, by prior agreement of the patient or the patient's agent, the patient is given no food or water and slowly dies of starvation and dehydration. In some cases the patient or family may request that the patient be given no food or nutrition, but be given fluids out of concern that even an unconscious patient may suffer from dehydration.

However, the administration of fluids can keep an unconscious patient alive for weeks, possibly more than a month. In either case the patient is unconscious and does not suffer from hunger or thirst or any other symptoms.

A few years ago I observed Edith N., a patient who was dying slowly of a rare form of cancer, with great pain and other indignities. Her physicians were slow to increase her morphine dosage, but after repeated urgings from the patient as well as her nurses, and after explaining the procedure to the family, the doctor in charge began an intravenous infusion of a barbiturate that provided total sedation and unconsciousness. The patient received no more fluids than were necessary to administer the sedative medicine, and no nourishment. She was peaceful and died three days after sedation began. Family members were distressed that the final dying phase took that long, but they were relieved to know their loved one was not suffering.

Justification for Terminal Sedation

Terminal sedation that leads to death through de-hydration and starvation is considered an acceptable practice because (1) the drug is administered to relieve suffering, and (2) a patient has the right to refuse life-sustaining therapy (fluids and nutrition, given intravenous-ly or through a tube placed in the stomach). Most physicians, however, are unfamiliar with using intravenous barbiturates and feel that for better dosage control they must hospitalize the patient, whereas they feel comfortable administering morphine drips in patients' homes. For this reason, terminal sedation with barbiturates is not nearly as widely practiced in the United States as is the morphine drip.

The extent to which terminal sedation shortens the dying process depends on when in the dying process the treatment is begun. If, for example, a patient were likely to die anyway within two days of starting the sedation, it may not shorten the dying process at all. On the other hand, if a patient probably has a month or two of life left when the sedation is begun, the dying process might be shortened by weeks or more than a month.

When first introduced, these two techniques—the morphine drip and terminal

TERMINAL sedation is a legal means of rendering a dying patient continuously and effectively unconscious for the purpose of complete elimination of suffering at the end of life.

sedation with barbiturates—were opposed by many who considered them forms of "killing." Although these techniques do require the involvement of physicians and do likely alter the time and means of dying, as physicians and medical ethicists say, "The disease, not the drug, kills the patient." This is, I believe, absolutely correct. The new language referring to these means of dying as "natural" may have the effect of hiding physicians' involvement in managing the process of dying, but by any rational analysis the disease, not the drug, has killed the patient. The linguistic mechanism has helped relieve much suffering, although it also has prevented the public from realizing how involved physicians are in managing the way we die.

IF WE ARE to have any meaningful say in how we die, the necessary first step is understanding something about the modern processes of dying. The methods of medically managing dying discussed in this chapter vary, but they have in common being new, unnatural processes unknown just fifty years ago. They are examples of the use of medical technologies and techniques, controlled and used by patients and their doctors, to alter the process of dying.

Summary

1. Dying is not an isolated event at the very end of life, but a process in which many events over our lifetime contribute to when and how we die.

2. Modern technologies prevent the older and often quicker methods of dying, such as from infectious diseases, and allow us to live longer so that ultimately we die of more chronic, debilitating diseases, such as cancer.

3. Physicians directly alter our dying processes by curing us of many previously fatal illnesses and by extending our lives after we have developed fatal conditions. Sometimes these

medical interventions result in extended dying with increased suffering.

4. The dying process is in some cases altered by medical methods of helping patients die with less suffering. These include

- non-resuscitation
- discontinuation of life-support therapy, including artificial ventilator, feeding tube or intravenous nourishment, essential drugs, kidney dialysis, pacemaker or heart defibrillator
- aggressive comfort care (most commonly, morphine drip)
- terminal sedation

· 3 ·

Advance Directives
Living Wills and Durable Powers
of Attorney

THE FIRST STEP in planning ahead is letting other people—your family and your doctors—know what course you would like to take when you are in the process of dying. In this chapter we will discuss advance directives, which can be a very good way of indirectly communicating your general plans for end-of-life medical care to any or all of your doctors, as well as anyone else you want to know of your plans. There are two types of advance directives. The first, a living will, is a general statement of your wishes or desires for end-of-life care. The second, a durable power of attorney for health care, is a mechanism for letting someone else make medical decisions for you if you become unable to do so yourself.

If you're not currently diagnosed with a terminal illness, it's not necessary to get into details with doctors about how you want to die. In fact, discussing specifics with your doctors when you're still relatively healthy probably won't do you any good in the long run and actually can work against you. If you are still relatively young, you may see doctors infrequently and not know any of them well. You may change insurance plans or move out of the area, or your doctor may stop working with your insurance plan. In addition, if you get into a big discussion with your doctors now about dying, they may think you're depressed or that you have a phobia about dying. Even if you're elderly you can't be sure which doctors you will be dealing with when you become fatally ill. But advance directives can communicate your general wishes to all medical providers as well as your family. This is why you need to get both. Now.

The Living Will

A *LIVING WILL* is a legal document, addressed to all your health care providers—doctors, nurses, physicians' assistants, physical therapists, counselors—that will be in your medical record wherever you go or whomever you see. Sometimes a living will is called a *health care directive,* or just an *advance directive.* It should express in clear terms your general desires about what you want and do not want if and when you become terminally ill.

How to Prepare a Living Will

You may, of course, simply write out your desires on a piece of paper, in your own language, but it would be better to type it, so people can read it. However, officialdom and legal correctness being what they are, most states require a specific form and may not honor your unofficial statement. Although anything is better than nothing, you are much better off using the official form, if only because doctors and health care personnel are more likely to ignore anything else, and statements not in your state's approved form may be deemed not legally valid.

YOUR LIVING WILL should specifically state the life-sustaining treatments you do or do not want. These should include resuscitation, use of an artificial ventilator, and artificial nutrition and hydration.

You can get a state-approved form for a living will from most doctors' offices, most health care facilities, or your city, county, or state department of health. (See the sample in appendix 1 for an example of a typical living will form.) You will need to sign the form in front of at least two people who can attest to its authenticity and its correctness with regard to your desires. These witnesses should not be related to you or mentioned in your will, and they may not be persons who might provide health services for you, such as your doctor or social worker.

What a Living Will Covers

Living wills address the big issues of how you want to direct your medical care should you become unable to do so. A lot of people use a living will to specify that if they are dying without hope of recovery and slip into a coma, they wish no therapy that will prolong their lives, such as feeding tubes, ventilators, or kidney dialysis. This means not starting any new life-sustaining treatment as well as stopping or withdrawing any such treatment already in place. In particular, living wills speak to the question of whether and how you want to be kept alive by medical treatment if you are unable to make decisions yourself.

Some living will forms ask for your specific direction with regard to certain procedures, such as whether you want artificially provided nutrition and hydration, or resuscitation if your heart stops. Most state-approved living will forms take you through the major issues in a way that you can understand and enable you to choose what you want. Most important, the wording on virtually all official forms asks your physicians and family to honor your directives. However, forms vary from state to state, and many do not have a full checklist of conditions or treatments for which you may want to give directives. A comprehensive living will form should contain the components listed below. If the form used by your state does not include some of these elements, you should feel free to add these in by hand. (We discuss particular elements in more detail below.) Here are the important components of a living will:

- A statement defining the medical conditions covered by the living will—for example: a terminal illness; a permanent unconscious condition
- A statement about whether and when to withhold or withdraw life-sustaining treatment that would

serve only to artificially prolong the process of dying

- A statement about whether and when to use CPR (resuscitation)
- A statement about whether and when you want artificial administration of food and fluids
- A statement requesting medicines to be administered in sufficient quantity to relieve suffering

What a Living Will Does for You

A living will is the best means of making a statement to medical professionals of your wishes for the use of life-prolonging medical care if you should become terminally ill or permanently unconscious and unable to make medical decisions. A patient close to dying may be heavily drugged or sedated to relieve pain and therefore unable to think clearly. Or the patient may be so fatigued or weakened she literally can't respond to questions from doctors about what she wants done. If doctors can't adequately communicate with a patient, or if they suspect a patient is not thinking clearly, they might be unwilling to go by what the

A LIVING WILL can prevent immense family conflict about your wishes for treatment if you become permanently unconscious or unable to make medical decisions.

patient seems to indicate under the extreme stress of the moment.

For example, suppose an elderly man has had a heart attack and is heavily medicated to relieve pain. Suppose also that there is almost no hope for recovery and the man's heart and lungs are so weak he is being kept alive by an artificial ventilator connected to a tube inserted into his windpipe, which means he cannot talk. Now, suppose the dying man understands all this and is able to scribble on a pad of paper, "I am ready to die. Turn off the ventilator."

The man's doctors may not honor his request, reasoning that there is a small possibility they can strengthen him and get him breathing on his own, at which time he will be glad they kept him alive. Or, and this happens commonly, someone in the family may say to the doctors, "Don't listen to him, he doesn't know what he's saying." This second-guessing of the patient may well lead to exactly what the man did not want—extended suffering until death. A living will makes your wishes clear, preventing second-guessing.

The Unconscious Patient

The need for a living will is even greater for a patient who becomes permanently or persistently unconscious because of a stroke or from brain damage due to an accident or other cause. In such a situation not only the patient's doctors but also her family may not know exactly how she would want to handle the medical treatment if she were able to direct it.

The major issue in the case of permanent unconsciousness is whether you would want the use of life-sustaining treatment withheld or withdrawn if, in the best medical judgment of your physicians, it would serve only to prolong the process of dying or staying alive for a long time in an unconscious condition. Some people would want no further treatment at this point, while others would want to be sure their doctors would continue all possible life-sustaining therapy. With luck you will never face this excruciating choice, but how you decide this issue could be the most important single factor in determining how you die.

The Use of Life-Prolonging Therapy

You should be sure that your living will specifies your directives for when and whether you want life-prolonging therapy. For example, people don't usually think of antibiotics as "life sustaining," but for a dying patient they may well be so; therefore, some people choose to write into their living will that antibiotics are included in the treatments they do not want if dying or permanently unconscious. You may write in any other specific treatment, such as kidney dialysis, that you think might be an issue in your particular case. The three types of life-sustaining treatments that you should be sure are explicitly stated, along with your choice as to whether you want them, are

1. Resuscitation
2. Use of an artificial ventilator
3. Artificial nutrition and hydration

In particular, if your state's form does not address the issue of artificial hydration and nutrition with a feeding tube or by intravenous therapy, you should write in your preference for whether you would want to be kept alive by this means, and under what conditions.

In a living will you also may make a general statement about your wishes, if you believe the form does not allow an adequate expression of them. You might say, for instance, "If I become incapable of directing my medical care and am terminally ill or permanently unconscious, I request treatment only for comfort and refuse any and all treatments that would prolong my life." If you wish, you may also state a desire not to go to a hospital or to a nursing home, but to die at home. Or, if you feel differently, you could say, "If I become incapable of making medical decisions, I request all possible medical treatment to keep me alive as long as possible."

In sum and substance, a living will is a directive to your physicians and family stating your wishes for how aggressively you want to be kept alive if you would in all probability die without life-sustaining treatment.

Adding a Doctor's Directive

If you want to be sure everyone knows exactly what treatments you would or would not want under different clinical situations such as (1) being in a coma, (2) having severe brain damage from a stroke or dementia as occurs with Alzheimer's Disease, or (3) being near death, write out your wishes on a separate sheet of paper. For each condition state whether you would or would not want major surgery, artificial feeding or hydration, an artificial respirator, antibiotics or blood transfusions, or other specific treatments.

Some physicians have forms called a "Doctor's Directive," or a "Medical Directive," on which you can do the same by checking your wishes for specific treatments given conditions under which you would not be able to make competent decisions. These forms or your statement give more specific directions to your surrogate decision maker, and you should sign and attach them to your advance directives as supplements.

The Limitations of Living Wills

Unfortunately, having a living will by itself may not set your course as you have directed. You need to be aware of two major limitations of living wills:

1. *Health care providers may be unaware of your advance directives.* You and your family are responsible for making sure that a copy of your living will is in your medical record for every physician or health care facility you use. There have been innumerable cases of a family member of an unconscious and dying patient telling a physician that the patient has a living will, but it isn't in the doctor's records and no one can find it. When they have to make important medical decisions your doctors can't wait while someone searches for your living will. Doctors can't take someone else's word for what you said in your advance directive.

2. *Even when physicians are aware of a living will and the directives in it, they will disregard it if they think they should act otherwise.* Suppose you have a living will in which you have stipulated no resuscitation and you have a sudden cardiac arrest. Even if the physician on the spot at the moment knows of the directives in your living will, her training and instinct may tell her to resuscitate you. She reasons that if you could understand the situation you would want to be resuscitated, despite what you wrote in your living will five years ago. Physicians act according to the training and rules of their profession, and they may view any patient's advance thinking and request as questionable and not binding at the moment of an emergency.

> **A LIVING WILL is a necessary first step in directing your medical care, but doctors will not honor your directives if they think they should do otherwise.**

A few years ago I was walking along a hospital corridor when I heard and saw a commotion a few doors ahead of me. A resuscitation was going on, with more equipment and people gathered than could fit into the patient's room. I noticed the patient's hospital chart on a rack just outside the room and opened it to see if I should try to get involved. The first page in the patient's record was a living will in which the patient specifically asked for no resuscitation. When I pointed this out to the doctor in charge, she said, "Yes, but she would have wanted it now because she was improving with the treatments."

In fact, attorneys advise physicians and hospitals to disregard living wills if they think the directive is wrong or inappropriate. There are reasons for this. If no family member or close friend is present to insist on the patient's directive, courts will generally uphold the physician who acts as she thinks best. In addition, if any family member or friend disagrees with the intent of the patient's directive or asks that it be disregarded, physicians or health care facilities are at legal risk in disregarding the family or friend and following the patient's directive. For example, if a friend present at the moment of cardiac arrest shouts at the physician, "Resuscitate," and the physician does not do so because of the patient's advance directive, that physician is at risk of a lawsuit. Physicians will do almost anything to avoid lawsuits.

In short, the going rule for doctors of always using the available treatment, such as resuscitation or artificial ventilation, can undermine your desires as stated in a living will.

The Risks of Not Having a Living Will

Although a living will may not be legally or medically binding, without one you're sunk in terms of asserting your wishes. If you haven't consented to stop life-prolonging treatment, you won't stand much chance of doctors doing it for you.

Recently, in the state of Virginia, Hugh Finn, forty-four years old, suffered severe brain damage in a car accident. After he had been in a nursing home for three and a half years in a persistent vegetative state (no ability to communicate, move independently, or feel pain), his wife requested that his feeding tube be removed because, she said, he had told her he would not want to live in this condition. However, other family members disputed what his wish would have been, and the case spun out of control with court appeals, an intervention by the governor of the state of Virginia to try to stop the removal of the tube, and a war of words between public groups and citizens opposing or supporting the removal of Hugh Finn's feeding tube. Ultimately, in 1998, the courts allowed withdrawal of the feeding tube, and Hugh Finn died several days later, but only after incredible conflict and emotional pain for many, particularly for family members on both sides of the controversy. A simple living will with a statement of Hugh Finn's general desires on the subject would have prevented all or most of that conflict.

Unfortunately, there have been many other sad cases like the Finn case, most of them unreported, in which a living will would have saved the immense suffering of family and friends when a loved one with no chance of recovery was not allowed to die. Don't take the chance of it happening to you. A living will is not always sufficient, but it's an essential first step.

If you want any assurance that your doctors will follow your wishes for end-of-life care, and that they will be allowed to do so by medical and legal authorities, you need a living will—now.

The Durable Power of Attorney for Health Care

AT THE SAME time that you obtain a living will form, get a form for durable power of attorney for health care, also called a *health care proxy*. This is the legal means by which you designate someone to make health care decisions for you if for any reason you should lose the capacity to do so. A durable (not ordinary) power of attorney for *financial* decisions—a document many people have heard of—is different from a durable power of attorney for health care.

THROUGH A durable power of attorney you may designate an agent who has legal standing to make health care decisions for you if you become unable to do so.

A durable power of attorney for financial decisions allows someone else to make financial decisions for you while you are away or not available, but it becomes invalid or nonoperative if you become impaired and unable to make decisions yourself. This is the opposite of a durable power of attorney for health care, under which the person you designate to make decisions for you can do so *only* if you become incapable of making medical decisions for yourself. Although it may be possible for you to combine the powers of attorney for health care and financial decisions in one document, it is not desirable.

Your Attorney-in-Fact

The person you designate to make health care decisions for you is called your *attorney-in-fact* and in some states may be called your *proxy, agent,* or *surrogate.* Your attorney-in-fact cannot be your physician or an employee of your physician or health care facility, such as a hospital or nursing home. The purpose of designating an attorney-in-fact is to enable this individual to make medical decisions for you just as you would have wanted to make them, knowing your wishes but of course using his or her discretion as to what is best for you in the particular situation.

You need an independent advocate precisely because the doctors or the facility, if left on their own, may make decisions contrary to your desires. If you regain consciousness, and regain competency to make your own decisions, your attorney-in-fact automatically loses power to make decisions for you, and that right reverts to you. If and when you are again incapable, the power of decision making again automatically transfers to your agent.

Choosing Your Attorney-in-Fact

Most people choose a close and trusted relative, such as spouse or child, to be their attorney-in-fact, but you should choose whoever you think would best represent you. Many elderly persons don't want to place the burden of medical decision making on an equally elderly spouse, and this is understandable. If such is your case, discuss your concern with your spouse or partner, and together talk out the issues and agree on someone agreeable to both of you. Choosing an attorney-in-fact can be a tricky, difficult task. A rift can occur if other family members disapprove of your choice. For example, if your eldest child lives far away and you think it would be best to appoint a younger child who lives nearby, discuss your reasoning with the eldest child before making your decision. In fact, talk it over with all members of your family, letting them know your reasons for your choice as well as your overall wishes.

John P. was an eighty-two-year-old man who had a living will and also had appointed his older son as his attorney-in-fact for health care. John told this son that under no circumstances did he want to be kept on life support if he developed an incurable condition. John thought he had things taken care of, but unfortunately he hadn't discussed these advance directives with his other son and his two daughters. During coronary bypass surgery, John suffered a heart attack followed by a stroke, and during recovery he developed severe pneumonia, for which he was treated with an artificial respirator. Two weeks later, when it was clear he would never recover from the damage to his heart, lungs, and brain, the son who was attorney-in-fact asked the doctors to remove all life-support treatments, including the respirator, in accordance with John's living will. However, when the two daughters, who had been keeping vigil in the hospital, learned of the request, they instructed the physicians to redouble their efforts to keep their father alive by all possible means, and they sought the support of their other brother, who chose to stay out of the argument. The doctors agreed with the daughters.

John lingered two more weeks in the intensive care unit before dying, and the two daughters and their older brother still do not speak to one another.

Two caveats about choosing your agent: First, you don't want an attorney-in-fact who is not trusted by other family members. You don't want a family dispute over what to do while you lie dying, connected to a ventilator. Try to choose someone who is trusted by the others to act on your behalf. It's in your interest to choose wisely so the process will work as smoothly as possible when you need it.

Second, if you know in advance that another family member may oppose your agent in carrying out one or more of your wishes, make sure that your agent cannot be challenged. For example, suppose you are firm in your desire that if you become permanently unconscious you want all life support stopped, including fluids and nutrition, but you have reason to believe that one family member would oppose that directive. In such a case, you should write on your durable power of attorney form, "If [name of the relative] opposes the decisions of my appointed agent, I direct my physicians and the courts to disregard [his/her] demands and to follow only the directives of my agent." If you have questions about this, see an attorney.

How to Prepare a Durable Power of Attorney for Health Care

As with a living will, you can create a durable power of attorney for health care by filling out a relatively simple form or document authorized by your state (see the example in appendix 1). With most durable power of attorney forms there are few decisions to make; these decisions are covered in your living will and it is the duty of your agent to carry them out. However, since some persons who have a durable power of attorney may not have a living will, the durable power of attorney forms of many states include many or most of the provisions covered by a living will. Even if the form accepted by your state duplicates your living will, be sure to fill it out completely so there can be no question of your intentions.

MAKE CLEAR TO other family members that your attorney-in-fact will have final authority to act on your behalf.

For instance, because the issue of artificial nutrition and hydration (intravenous or tube feeding) remains controversial, in some states an attorney-in-fact may not be able to refuse or stop life-sustaining feeding without a clear written directive from the patient. Your state's durable power of attorney form may have a place for you to give your wish on this specific issue. If you want to be absolutely sure there is no mistake about your wishes, you may write on the durable power of attorney form any or all of the specific directives you have listed in your living will.

It may seem unnecessary to have a living will if you have a durable power of attorney form that lists all the types of treatment you do or do not want. But it is best to have both; the living will is more accepted as your declaration or directive, while the durable power of attorney is the legal document that allows your agent to make decisions on your behalf.

Some patient-advocacy organizations have created forms that combine a living will and durable power of attorney and provide for more choices about specific treatments (see appendix 1). Some of these forms also include religious or philosophical statements and expressions of love and caring to family and friends, whom you can name on the form. Although these forms can be helpful, be sure any form you use is accepted by the state in which you live. If you are unsure about whether the form you want to use is valid, call your state health department to find out.

What to Include

A comprehensive durable power of attorney form should contain the components listed below. If the form used by your state does not include some of these elements, you should feel free to add these yourself.

- The name of your attorney-in-fact, plus (optional) an alternate attorney-in-fact

- A granting of power to your attorney-in-fact to make decisions and to give informed consent on your behalf if you are unable to make decisions

- A statement about whether and when to withhold or withdraw life-sustaining treatments or procedures, including resuscitation

- A declaration about whether and when you want artificial administration of food and fluids

- Any other specific instructions you may wish to write in, such as whether you want to be treated with a pacemaker, an artificial ventilator, or antibiotics

In many states you must have the durable power of attorney form notarized. You may cancel, add to, or change a living will or durable power of attorney at any time, so you are not bound to them. In fact, as with an ordinary will, it's a good idea to update your advance directives every five years or so.

Legal Status of Durable Power of Attorney

In contrast to a living will, a durable power of attorney generally does stand up in court. If your attorney-in-fact for health care makes a decision on your behalf that is consistent with your written advance directive, and with what other family and friends vouch as your wish, a physician or health care facility not honoring the decision is liable in a lawsuit. However, your attorney-in-fact for health care can be challenged for making decisions on which your prior intent is not clear. This was the problem in the case of Hugh

A DURABLE power of attorney stands up legally, particularly when the agent's decisions are consistent with directives contained in the patient's living will.

Finn, who had a legal guardian entitled to make medical decisions for him. When the guardian wanted to pull out Finn's feeding tube, a lengthy and nasty dispute followed precisely because Mr. Finn had no advance directive with regard to his wishes on the point, thus opening the way for others to challenge the guardian's decision as not consistent with Finn's wishes.

REGARDLESS OF WHETHER dying patients are able to make meaningful medical decisions to the end, advance directives are by far the best means of directing their process of dying. In general, the use of advance directives reduces unwarranted use of futile medical treatments without decreasing quality of life.

But it's not enough to just have a living will and a durable power of attorney. If we want these directives to work we must be sure all our doctors know about these documents. We must get copies of both these forms into all the medical records of each medical office we visit and every medical institution (hospital, nursing home, rehabilitation center) where we have been a patient and may possibly return. We must give a copy of each to our spouse or partner and to each adult child, as well as to any trusted friend who is likely to be nearby if or when we need these documents. And we must discuss with them the reasons for our decisions.

We must tell these people to be sure the necessary health care personnel are aware of our advance directives if and when our condition calls for it.

Summary

1. A living will is the best means of making a statement to medical professionals of how aggressively you want to be kept alive with life-prolonging medical care if you should become terminally ill or permanently unconscious and unable to make medical decisions.

2. To prepare your living will (sometimes called a health care directive), get an approved form from your doctor's office, health care facility, or city, county, or state department of health.

3. In your living will, be sure there are specific statements regarding your wishes for resuscitation and continuation or withdrawal of life-sustaining treatments (such as nutrition and hydration, ventilators, and antibiotics) in case you develop a terminal illness or permanent unconsciousness. Add a "doctor's directive" if you wish.

4. Because physicians might disregard your directives and others can challenge specific directives in your living will, get a durable power of attorney for health care. Forms for these also are available from your doctor's office, health care facility, or city, county, or state health department. On this form name an attorney-in-fact, or agent, who will have strong legal standing to make medical decisions for you if you become unconscious or unable to make decisions.

5. Choose someone for your attorney-in-fact who knows your wishes and will faithfully represent you according to the directives in your living will. Make it clear to other family members that your agent will have final authority to act on your behalf.

6. Get copies of both these forms into all the medical records of each medical office you visit and every medical institution (hospital, nursing home, rehabilitation center) where you have been a patient and may possibly return.

7. Give a copy of each to your spouse or partner and to each adult child, as well as to any trusted friend who is likely to be nearby if or when you need these documents. Tell these people to be sure the necessary health care personnel are aware of your advance directives and have copies, if your condition calls for it.

· 4 ·

Talking to
Important People

THE NEXT STEP in planning for a peaceful death is talking to people who will be important in carrying out your wishes: your doctors and your loved ones. You need to do this for the same reasons you need advance directives—events can creep up on you, or happen suddenly, and talking to important people in advance of a medical emergency or disability is absolutely essential to effective planning.

Talking to Your Doctor

AT THIS JUNCTURE, before you are terminally ill, it's not crucial to talk to your doctor in detail about how you want to die (in fact, as we discuss below, being too specific or detailed can work against you). Your advance directives will carry a lot more weight with your doctor than you will verbally, before you have a terminal illness at least. As mentioned in the previous chapter, most people who make out living wills do so to avoid or to withdraw life-sustaining treatment if the outlook is hopeless, and if a doctor knows you have an advance directive she will probably assume this is your desire. If, on the other hand, you want to be sure you get all possible treatments to sustain life whatever medical condition you may have, be sure your doctor understands this.

I do not mean to dissuade you from speaking your mind to your doctor about specific end-of-life decisions now, when you are healthy as a horse or at least not seriously ill, but be aware of the limitations of doing so. Many physicians consider "thoughts about dying" to be evidence of depression. I know physicians who have prescribed antidepressants for healthy patients who have wanted to talk about dying. Of course, you can and should precede a discussion about dying with the explanation that you are simply looking ahead, or planning. Most doctors will accept this, but, unless you are terminally ill, they may think it is not appropriate.

A neighbor recently asked me about a drug her doctor had prescribed. When I told her it was an antidepressant, she was both embarrassed and angry. I asked her what she had said to the doctor to make him prescribe this drug and she said, "Nothing; it was a routine checkup." But she then added that she had taken the opportunity to talk about what she wanted done if she were to die or become fatally ill.

Broaching the Subject with Your Doctor

Despite these potential problems, it's not a bad idea to have a brief discussion about your general views on the subject with your doctor. An early discussion with your doctor can give you some insight into her general philosophy about end-of-life care, how aggressive she would be in pushing life-prolonging treatment, and whether she would share end-of-life decision making with you.

You may get a vague answer to a question such as how vigorously your doctor would treat you if you lapsed into a terminal coma. Physicians like to know the specifics of clinical conditions and are highly reluctant to say what they would do without knowing all the details, because they really don't know how they might react to a situation until they get into it. Doctors also know that although they give a yes or no answer to a question such as, "If I'm dying and hooked to a ventilator will you disconnect it?" they might act differently if that situation ever arises for you. Nevertheless, if you assure your doctor you aren't trying to pin her down or get a commitment, she might give you some indication of where she is on the overall scale of aggressiveness in treatment for terminally ill, incurable patients.

Some patients seek out physicians known to be willing to forgo aggressive end-of-life treatment and attempt to establish a relationship with them. A few healthy patients seek out doctors for the sole purpose of asking for a commitment to participate in assisted suicide or some other form of aid-in-dying at an unspecified time in the future. This can create a problem for the doctor, even if she is sympathetic to your goals, because she doesn't want to be committed in advance to a certain course, particularly aid-in-dying, and she also doesn't want to develop a reputation for catering to patients with certain life philosophies or desires. Most physicians want to serve a broad range of patients and want to be able to do so in their own way without advance agreements or promises about end-of-life care that they may regret later on. A doctor might say she is open to all considerations at appropriate times, but this is as far as any physician should go.

I recommend that you simply inform your doctor of your desires, generally and without specific requirements. This has the dual advantage of informing the doctor of your wishes while not putting her on the spot or asking for a commitment.

For example, you might say, "If I am incurably ill and dying, I don't want any treatment that would prolong my life. I just want medicines to keep me comfortable and out of pain." Chances are the doctor won't respond other than to acknowledge that she heard you and will try to do her best for you if you get to the end.

PHYSICIANS LIKE to know the specifics of clinical conditions and are highly reluctant to say what they would do without knowing all the details.

But she will probably make a note of it in your record. You've made a statement that will count later on if the issue comes up. If you're not satisfied with her response, you could add, "Are you willing to work with me in this way?" or, "Does this fit within your style of practice?"

Or you could just say, "Here is a copy of my living will, which spells out my wishes if and when it comes to that." If the doctor surprises you and responds with questions about specific end-of-life conditions or treatments, get into it. Otherwise, know that for most patients a living will is an expression of not wanting excessive or heroic treatments at the end and that your doctor will get at least that much of your message.

Asking About Aid-in-Dying

If it is extremely important to you to know well in advance whether a physician is likely to honor a request for a form of physician aid-in-dying, such as assisted suicide, you could say, "If I become terminally and incurably ill, I may ask you to give me pills to help me die." Or, "If I become terminally ill and am suffering, I will want to have the option of assisted dying." On the other hand, if you have the opposite philosophy for end-of-life medical care, you could say, "If someday I am dying, I would want you to give me every medical treatment available to keep me alive as long as possible, even if most doctors think it might not work."

These statements are unequivocal and understandable to any physician. They make a statement about you, but they don't demand an answer. If you get one, fine; then you know where your doctor stands on the issue. If she answers, "Well, let's see when the time comes," don't try to read much into it. It's not a commitment one way or the other. A thoughtful doctor might respond to your statement by asking questions in order to understand better your concerns and why you seek a particular plan for end-of-life treatment. Or it's possible the doctor might be opposed to your plan and want to know your thinking for purposes of dissuading you from your implied request. Any talk arising from this sort of statement will give you some insight into how your doctor might react if you get into a specific end-of-life condition and will also serve as the opening for later discussions if and when they are needed.

Talking to Your Family and Friends

IN THE LONG run, letting your family and close friends know your wishes for end-of-life care is probably the most important part of planning for a peaceful death because these are the people you will be most dependent upon for helping you fulfill your wishes for peaceful dying. If you are dying and not capable of making decisions, almost certainly you will have family or friends looking after you and interacting with your health care providers. Just as you must make out a living will and durable power of attorney

IF YOU GIVE your family enough advance notice of your wishes for end-of-life care, they will almost always support you.

because sudden events may mean you cannot make medical decisions, for the same reason your family and friends must know in advance your wishes for end-of-life care. They can read your advance directives, but there's nothing like hearing it directly from you.

Talking to Everyone Important to You

Discuss your advance directives with as many family members as possible. A single family member could undermine your wishes just because she or he has not been aware of them.

I once saw this exact thing happen with Harry V., a patient who had been on a ventilator for two weeks, with no chance of survival. He was seventy-three years old and had always been a healthy, hardworking man. But he had smoked and developed lung cancer. The doctors were able to remove the tumor, but they also had to remove most of one lung. Harry did fairly well for about six months but then began to have one infection after another in his remaining lung. Soon he had to be hospitalized and put on a ventilator to stay alive. After Harry was on the ventilator for two weeks, it became clear to his doctors, and to him, that he had no chance of survival. He was fully able and competent to make decisions, and he requested removal of the ventilator, knowing it would mean the end. All the family who had been in on the discussions with Harry agreed at a conference to do it the next morning. Just before the appointed time, a twenty-four-year-old grandson arrived at the hospital and insisted, "You can't do that to my grandfather." The doctors and the family were unwilling to act against the grandson's wish, and Harry continued to suffer on the ventilator another five days before dying, while the rest of the family looked on helplessly. This happened because no one had talked to the grandson.

Let your views and wishes be known among your family and friends. Give them time to understand your wishes and work out any disagreements. Give them a copy of your living will and durable power of attorney for health care and explain your directives to them. Tell them why you would or would not want to be kept alive by tube feeding if you were in a permanent coma, or at what point or under what conditions you would not want to be resuscitated.

If Someone Disagrees with Your Plan

If they disagree with your requests for whatever reason, tell them they don't have to agree but that it's what you want. It is particularly important to air potential disagreements that might disrupt your plans or the emotional well-being of family or friends. If, for example, you are interested in or contemplate using physician-assisted suicide, you don't have to tell everyone you know, but you should discuss this with one or two of your closest family members or friends. Such a proposed course would have a profound effect on your family, and you must give them the chance to consider it and to explore your reasons for wanting it.

If one or more of them disagree with your desires, don't panic or respond angrily. Keep in mind, the best way for your loved ones to deny the possibility of you ever dying is to oppose any of your plans for dying, especially if they involve shortening your life from what is technologically possible. They probably haven't thought it through like you have; they might simply be reacting to the thought of losing you someday. Once they recover from the shock and understand your wishes there may be no true disagreement.

Discussing your advance directives with family and friends is the best means you have of checking the reality and validity of your choices. If you find opposition, you need to examine your reasoning as well as the reasoning of those who oppose your plans. But take heart. By the end most family members will accept your decisions if they are convinced they represent your true ideals and wishes. Start the discussion now.

If You Are a Family Member or Friend

IF YOU ARE a family member or friend of someone who has spoken to you about their advance planning for dying, do not immediately assume that your relative or friend is dying! You can check that possibility by asking, "I assume this is strictly for long-term planning purposes?" or words to that effect. Try to understand that her planning for dying is a prudent form of insurance.

Your job first and foremost is to listen and to be attentive to her wishes and concerns. Listen and ask questions, but don't begin by telling her what to do or not do. Remem-ber, by the time she has begun talking to you or asking you to witness an advance directive she probably has looked into the matter carefully and discussed it with other people, including one or more physicians. You can help to develop the checklist of conditions and treatments included in her advance directives. Ask her, for example,

"Have you thought about whether you would want resuscitation or tube feeding if you are in an auto accident and are permanently unconscious or have no ability to think?" You might also be sure she has named an attorney-in-fact for health care decisions and has discussed her personal philosophy or wishes with that person.

If your relationship allows, you can ask about her deepest concerns or fears. You could ask, "What is the single worst-case situation you want to avoid?" You might also ask whom she most wants to protect. For example, is she most

IF YOU ARE a family member or friend of someone who has spoken to you about their advance planning for dying, do not immediately assume that your relative or friend is dying!

concerned about her equally elderly spouse and the burden she might be to him if she became incapacitated? If so, you might be able to lead your friend to consider or explore arrangements for future nursing home or hospice care, in order to alleviate or resolve her concerns about caregiving if she became incapacitated.

If You Disagree with the Plan

If you have serious misgivings or objections to one or more of the requests in her living will, or to the person that she intends to appoint as attorney-in-fact, say so. Better to talk about it now than later when things may be moving quickly. If you are a child of the prospective patient, you may feel she is making plans to depart more quickly or willingly than you desire. In all likelihood this is simply your reaction to the thought of losing a parent, but keeping your feelings to yourself is not in her best interest or yours. Expressing your fears or concerns is a way of saying you care about her.

If your relative or friend says that when the time comes she will seek physician-assisted suicide if in her judgment it is necessary, inquire as to her reasons. Try to understand what she wants and why. Remain open so she will come back to you to discuss these issues again, if and when it becomes necessary.

You can best help your relative or friend by being supportive without imposing your values on her. Of course, if you have grave concerns about her plans, you must state your position. React the way you would want her to react if you were approaching her for the same reason.

Summary

Talking to Your Doctor

1. When you are still well, you need not explore issues of dying with your doctor in any detail. However, you should let your doctor know, in general terms, your desires for end-of-life care. You can do this best by presenting her with your living will.

2. If you feel strongly about a specific measure, such as assisted dying or maximal treatment to the end, find out if your doctor is opposed to this course and ask for enough of a response to determine whether she will consider supporting you, but do not ask for a commitment in advance.

Talking to Your Family and Friends

1. You may need your family and friends to help you at the end, so share your wishes for end-of-life care with them.

2. Let as many family members and friends know your wishes as is reasonable, and discuss any disagreements. A single family member who disagrees can block your plans at the end.

3. If you give your family enough time to consider your wishes for end-of-life care, they will almost always give you the support you need.

Suggestions for Family Members or Friends

1. If a family member or friend approaches you to discuss plans for dying some day in the future, think of her planning as a prudent form of insurance.

2. Listen carefully and reserve judgment. React the way you would want her to react if you were approaching her for the same reason.

3. If you have objections to specific plans, say so but keep the dialogue open.

4. Urge her to speak to her physician and to other important family members if she hasn't done so.

5. Be sure that she has a living will and a durable power of attorney, and get copies for yourself.

PART TWO

Taking Charge After the Diagnosis

In this part, we'll discuss how to:

1. Talk to your doctor.

2. Ask for a general prognosis for the disease.

3. Understand the inability of physicians to give you a personalized prediction of outcome.

4. Research your condition and familiarize yourself with standard medical statistics and what they mean.

5. Study and choose treatment options on the basis of your life situations and beliefs.

6. Choose a trusted doctor to be your spokesperson for major medical decisions.

7. Discuss the end-of-life options of aid-in-dying with your doctors.

8. Discuss your condition and plans with your family.

· 5 ·

Learning the Diagnosis

IN ANCIENT TIMES physicians had scarcely any tools with which to cure their patients or even to prolong their lives. But even then it was very important for both doctors and patients to know the nature of the disease afflicting a dying patient. The diagnosis of the disorder gave the community an understanding of the workings of the gods, and it gave an individual patient an understanding of her place in the universe and why she was dying.

Modern people are no different. When we become ill we want an explanation for what is wrong with us. And now we have an additional need to know the diagnosis— it is the starting point for controlling our process of dying. In this chapter we will talk about how to learn the diagnosis and what it means.

Why You Need to Know

IF YOU BECOME ill with an incurable or ultimately fatal disease, you have some serious talking to do with your doctor, family, and friends. But before you can talk to anyone you need to learn about your condition. And, as we all know, doctors don't always tell patients the whole of the bad news.

Secrecy

Just twenty-five or thirty years ago it was the rule rather than the exception for a doctor to withhold from a patient the actual diagnosis of a fatal illness, at least for a time, in the belief that to tell the whole truth would "devastate" the patient. Family members often pleaded with the doctor not to tell the patient because "it would kill him to know." Patients who did learn of their terminal illness often asked their physician not to tell the spouse or the family, for similar reasons. About twenty years ago the wife of a patient of mine accosted me in the hall and said, "Please, don't tell my husband the diagnosis. It would kill him." When I went to see the patient, who was alone in the exam room, he said to me, "I know I have cancer. But please, whatever you do, don't tell my wife; it would kill her to find out."

The paternalism of "helping" patients by keeping knowledge from them was in keeping with the beliefs and customs of the time. Although today it seems downright dishonest for a physician not to tell a patient that she has an incurable and fatal illness, back then, the withholding of information had little effect on the outcome and the process of dying because medical treatment could do little to alter the course of the fatal disease. Whether right or wrong, the practice of not telling the patient everything was based on the prevailing belief that a dying patient would be better off, or happier, being unaware of his condition.

Choosing Your Treatment(s)

Things are different now. If you contract a fatal illness in this day and age your process of dying is no longer a matter of "fate" or entirely out of your hands. Far from it. The process of dying will be spread out over multiple treatments involving many medical decisions, sometimes numbering in the hundreds. You will frequently face the option of choosing from among two or more equally "correct" treatments. Your choice will, in greater or lesser part, determine the course of your illness and how you ultimately die. This is why being unaware of your condition is unacceptable if you want to participate in setting your course of dying.

On the other hand, if you wish for others—physicians for the most part—to make these choices for you, you may do so by default. It is, after all, the time-honored method to ask no questions and let the doctors do as they choose. However, if you want any input into the course of your fatal illness you must have sufficient information. And the bedrock of necessary information is the diagnosis.

The Diagnosis

FORTUNATELY, OVER THE past two decades physicians have shed a lot of their paternalism and don't as often "protect" patients from the diagnosis of a fatal illness.

Medical ethicists insist on "truth telling" about diagnoses, by which they mean that doctors should not withhold information from their patients. The great majority of physicians today believe it is absolutely essential for a patient to be well informed about her condition in order to participate in the treatment. Many physicians are actually unwilling to treat patients who are not fully informed about their diagnosis and the various possible outcomes of the proposed treatments.

> **MOST PHYSICIANS today believe it is absolutely essential for a patient to understand her condition well enough to participate in the treatment.**

Today a bewildering array of tests and treatments are available, many of them unpleasant if not toxic or painful, and doctors need your understanding and cooperation to get them done. Nevertheless, despite the new ethics of truth telling and the need for your cooperation, many physicians still "go slow" in breaking the news, and they might bring it out in steps spaced out over two or more visits.

Bad News Is Hard to Give

Giving bad news is not an easy task for physicians. You may think that dealing with disease all the time hardens doctors and enables them to broach any subject without feeling uneasy. Not so. Your doctor may not have had time to develop a very deep relationship with you and so may not have a personal stake in the problem, but very few physicians can break the news of terminal illness without feeling true discomfort. The insensitive and detached demeanor some physicians have when they break the bad news may seem like reprehensible bedside manners, but for some it is a defense mechanism, a very human way of coping with sadness. Physicians do become desensitized to the sight of blood, or even to a cardiac arrest, but there is nothing in medical training and experience that diminishes the human aversion to having to tell someone they have a fatal condition. In fact, the pain of giving the bad news may increase with time and experience.

There is no good or easy way to give bad news, and physicians often rationalize not giving you the diagnosis by telling themselves they need more information and that you need more time to be "ready" to hear the news. Sometimes the family pressures the doctor to withhold the bad news; sometimes the doctor chooses to wait until the diagnosis is absolutely clear, rather than just 80 to 90 percent certain. Although lengthy withholding of information is now relatively rare, for these seemingly innocent and well-intentioned reasons a patient may go weeks or months before learning the real nature of her illness.

Delays in Diagnosis

Sometimes a lengthy period of testing must occur before the diagnosis becomes certain. This testing period is often marked by ambiguous statements from doctors and pleas for time to do even more testing to get more information. The process of narrowing down to the one sure diagnosis goes on, properly and necessarily, and it takes time. Although most physicians are actually very good at expediting such a medical work-up, and delays may give both patient and physician time to ease into the bad news, as a patient you can't afford to lose months of planning. You need to know as soon as possible what is happening, because events may preempt your ability to direct your care.

A physician friend of mine, Dr. L., had a patient who had experienced bloating and discomfort in the abdomen for a month. Although Dr. L. had reasons to suspect cancer, she didn't want to alarm her patient by mentioning the "C" word without any evidence. Dr. L. ordered an examination of the bowel with a long, flexible scope. Because this is usually a safe procedure, Dr. L. believed she could wait to inform her patient until after the test had confirmed or repudiated her tentative diagnosis. Unfortunately, during the procedure, bleeding occurred and Dr. L. had to rush her patient to the operating room for emergency surgery to stop the bleeding. During surgery, Dr. L.'s patient suffered a stroke, and he died two months later, never regaining consciousness.

Dealing with Uncertainty

Today more physicians are telling their patients of all the possibilities before the diagnosis is known for sure, but they must balance the benefit of giving information with the disadvantage of possibly giving misleading information. In situations like this, patients must accept some uncertainty and even some risk of emotional distress in order to be forewarned of possibilities. If there's any hint of something seriously wrong, or you want a better explanation of what is happening, ask the doctor for more information.

Insist on it. In this day and age, physicians are quite accustomed to patients challenging them on all sorts of levels, and as long as you don't challenge their professional competency, virtually all doctors will respond if you ask. If you've any reason to think the doctor may be withholding possible bad news, just say, "I appreciate the difficulty in knowing things with 100 percent certainty, but I want to know everything you can tell me, however uncertain, even if it's bad news."

A lot of the reluctance doctors have about sharing diagnoses before they are 100 percent certain results from the difficulty most patients have in processing information of an uncertain nature. Think of how much trouble you may have in hearing a tentative or unconfirmed diagnosis. Will you hear correctly what the doctor is saying? Will you overreact to a possibility rather than a certainty? If the diagnosis is uncertain, you must be prepared to live for a while with nagging uncertainty.

A DELAY IN knowing that you may have a serious illness may rob you of your ability to direct your care if complications occur.

However difficult the news may be, getting it is essential to taking charge of directing your medical care. Therefore, don't let doctors hedge or delay in telling you what they know or suspect.

Understand that they often are distressed over what they know, but let them know you are willing to live with some uncertainty. Tell them it's your body, your life, and that you need to know. Physicians are well aware of the "need to know" for their own purposes, and if you tell them you also have a need to know, they will share information with you. A good way to open a physician to a full and frank discussion is to say, "I'm not afraid of the truth. Please tell me everything you know." When physicians hear this, they'll talk.

Summary

1. Even though physicians deal frequently with death and dying, it is emotionally difficult for them to give you bad news.

2. Physicians may delay in giving a fatal diagnosis until very certain of it, partly because of patients' difficulty in dealing with uncertainty.

3. Since time is important for sufficient planning, ask for more information if you think your physician is withholding information from you.

4. Be prepared to deal with some uncertainty. Tell your doctor you want to know the truth.

· 6 ·

Talking to Your Doctor
After the Diagnosis

Iᴛ's ɪᴍᴘᴏssɪʙʟᴇ ᴛᴏ get bad news without its being a blow. Perhaps this is what people of the previous generation were trying to avoid when physicians and family told a lot of little white lies to avoid the hurt of the truth. Presumably, if a patient received a series of vague and small clues over a period of a year or so, by the time she heard the actual diagnosis (if ever) she would have become resigned to something bad and it wouldn't come as a shock.

But doing it that way doesn't work today. You have to get started early in learning about your disease so that you can share in important medical decisions. In this chapter we will talk about all the things you need to talk about with your doctors.

Absorbing the Diagnosis

Iɴ ᴏʀᴅᴇʀ ᴛᴏ understand what a specific diagnosis means, we first need to define some terms. A *fatal* disease is one that in its natural, untreated course will be fatal. Cancer, heart attacks, and pneumonia can all be fatal if untreated, but some cancers, many heart attacks, and most cases of pneumonia are *not* fatal if medically treated. In common medical usage, a fatal disease is one that is usually or often fatal, but not necessarily so. It is therefore more accurate to say a disease is *potentially fatal*, rather than fatal. For example, leukemia is often fatal, but with treatment some patients are cured. Other patients with potentially fatal cancers, for instance prostate cancer, may never be cured but their disease is controllable with treatment for years or decades. If such a patient dies years later of another cause, for example, the prostate cancer will have been incurable but not fatal. Therefore, if you are diagnosed with a fatal disease it does *not* mean that you will die of the disease. For most fatal diseases some cures are possible, and for others reasonably long life is possible without a cure.

In medical terms, however, a *terminal* illness means a fatal disease that has advanced beyond the point of reasonable hope for a cure, and it usually means the patient has less than six months to live. Unfortunately, even physicians may misuse these terms, particularly by speaking of a "terminal" disease when they mean a potentially fatal disease that has some chance of cure. So if your doctor confuses or alarms you with terms, ask for clarification.

When You First Hear the Bad News

Even if you have been suspecting bad news, when you learn that you have a potentially fatal illness, you may need some time to sort through the emotional wreckage. Take time to settle down so that you will be able to react rationally in planning for the future. When you first hear the news, don't hesitate to ask the doctor everything that comes to your mind, but don't think you have to get it all right away. It's a lot to absorb. It is widely assumed by physicians, and studies tend to support this assumption, that the average patient understands and absorbs about half of what he is told in a typical encounter with a doctor. This is especially true when the patient is getting bad news, and it remains a potent reason for having a clear-minded relative or friend accompany you on your visit to the doctor, particularly when you know you will be discussing important matters. The doctor may push to get started with treatments as soon as possible, but in most cases there should be time for you to absorb the information and come back another day (you'll have to come back anyway) to talk about long-term plans.

When you are leaving the doctor's office after learning your diagnosis, you may ask for another appointment within a few days to discuss things in more detail. If your doctor has fifteen- or twenty-minute appointment slots, and you think this will not be enough, ask for a thirty-minute appointment. Say something such as, "Doctor, I'm confused and worried about my condition, and I'd like enough time at our next visit to go over a lot of questions I have, and I know my wife (or daughter, or friend) who will be with me will have questions, also." Most doctors don't mind doing this if they know you are filling an otherwise empty slot in their schedule, so they will have time enough to talk.

Participating in Decisions

Some patients simply do not want to talk very much about their medical condition or become involved in medical decision making. These patients usually say something like, "You're the doctor; you make the decision." The desire to defer to the doctor exists in patients of all backgrounds—rich or poor, urban or rural. It's a natural form of denial, and of hoping to be able to shift responsibility to a supreme healer, or at least to an "expert." I've had patients tell me, "When I take my car to the mechanic, I expect him to do what is necessary. When I see a doctor, I don't want to be asked to make medical decisions; that's the doctor's job." This approach is emotionally or personally best for some people and may work well for them. However, it is a little like letting a travel agent dictate where and when you'll take your vacation.

> **IF YOU DEFER all decisions to your doctor, she, not you, will control your dying process.**

If you defer all decisions to your doctor, he, not you, will control your dying process. If you want to be involved in directing this process, you must be involved in decisions, starting now. Get accustomed to shared decision making with your doctors from the beginning, since asserting your-self later may be more difficult. Shared decision making means a well-informed patient discussing treatment options or proposals with his doctor, with each using the input of the other in coming to a mutually respectful medical decision.

The three main steps to getting involved in the decision-making process are

1. Learn about your disease
2. Discuss options for treatment
3. Choose your treatments

Learning About Your Disease

WHETHER YOU START immediately or at the next visit, you have to learn all you can about the diagnosis and prognosis. Since the diagnosis may be unfamiliar to you, write it down. Ask the doctor as much as you want to know about exactly what this illness is, and what it does. Ask about the *pathophysiology* of the disease, which is how the disease alters the structure and functioning of organs. Know where the disease is in your body, where it might spread, what it does, and how it might affect your entire body. You'll need a reasonable understanding of the pathophysiology in order to understand how treatments work, and the possible limitations of treatments. Remember, though, that it took your doctor years to learn about your disease, so you can't acquire all his understanding in one visit. In most cases, you'll have plenty of time to learn all you want to know and are capable of absorbing.

Don't hesitate to ask your doctor to explain things thoroughly: one of the most important functions of a physician is to inform patients about illnesses or diseases. In fact, the word doctor comes from the Latin *docere*, which means "to teach." To be sure, many doctors are very busy, but all doctors know their duty to teach patients, and even the busiest and most tight-lipped will do it if you ask them to schedule the time for it.

The Prognosis

Also, right away, at your first full discussion, ask about the *prognosis,* which is the doctor's forecast of the course of the disease. The prognosis includes how long you are likely to live given the best treatment available and what is likely to happen along the way. Your doctor will probably hedge at this point, because the course of any disease is unpredictable and variable from person to person. But the doctor can tell you what to expect in general terms. I suggest you say something like, "From your experience, doctor, describe the average course of this disease from now to the end."

ONE OF THE most important functions of a physician is to inform or teach patients, so don't hesitate to ask your doctor about your disease.

Recognize that your asking about survival can bring unwanted answers if you are not prepared for full disclosure. In general, patients with terminal illnesses, at least in the early stages, are more optimistic than objective medical assessments warrant. As an approach to illness, a positive attitude anchored by hope is therapeutic, but you must temper unbridled hope with medical reality, as emotionally unsatisfactory as that may be. Hope is a powerful stimulant and support and may even produce a better response to treatment, but false or unsubstantiated hope often generates greater suffering for patient and family through unrealistic expectations of treatments.

For any given disease, your predicted survival time will depend on many factors. Some of these include (1) how early in its course the disease was detected (the earlier a disease like cancer is discovered the better the chance of cure or a longer survival), (2) whether you have other conditions such as diabetes or anemia, (3) your age, and (4) whether you are otherwise in good health. Doctors don't like to offer estimates of how long a patient may live, particularly early in the course of a fatal disease, because of the great individual natural variability in survival and because of great individual variability in response to treatment. A doctor who gives a specific time of probable survival, such as eight months, or three years, knows the chances of being correct are very unlikely, and so instead he will speak of survival in ranges of months or years, such as six to ten months, or two to four years.

Understanding Survival Statistics

A great deal of statistical information exists in the medical literature about how long patients survive with specific diseases; most physicians either know these statistics or can get them easily. Specialists in a particular disease know survival statistics very well for that disease. Doctors can't give you, as an individual, a precise survival time, but they can give you your probabilities or chances of survival.

For example, you may be quoted a 50 percent chance of living three years, or a 10 percent chance of living ten years. Keep in mind, these figures are based on the outcomes of other patients who had the same disease, but they had it before you and so may not have had access to newer treatments. A 50 percent probability of living three years means that, in the recent past, 50 percent of patients with this disease lived less than three years and 50 percent lived longer than three years (see table 2). Some might have lived only three months, and some may have lived eight or nine years. For your purposes this may not seem very exact or satisfactory, but given the impossibility of predicting for a single patient, this is the way your doctor will present the information to you.

TABLE 2

Example of Difference Between Survival and Cure
(Disease X)

Years after Treatment	Survival Rate	Cure Rate
1	90%	10%
2	80%	10%
5	15%	10%

Note: In this example all the cures were in the first year, and most of the patients who survived 5 years had been cured.

Ask for survival statistics. Keep in mind that any survival figure you may receive is subject to change, or updating, over the course of your illness. That is, a year after your diagnosis, and after repeat testing to assess the course of your disease, your doctor may say the original survival prognosis was too bleak and the outlook is now better, or it could go the other way. Updated survival outlook depends on how your body reacts to the disease and to treatment for it. Also, new treatments may improve the survival outlook.

Cure Vs. Survival

It is easy to be confused by how doctors speak about survival statistics because they sometimes use the term "cure" when they are speaking about "survival." Cure means total elimination or eradication of the disease, whereas survival refers to how long a person lives, with or without a cure. For many diseases, such as advanced heart disease or some cancers, there is never a cure although there can be long survival (see table 3).

Unfortunately, some doctors use the two words interchangeably by saying, for instance, "The five-year cure rate is 50 percent," when what they really mean is that the five-year survival rate is 50 percent. For example, if only 10 percent of patients with a certain disease live for five years without treatment, but 50 percent of patients live for five years with treatment, some doctors may refer to a patient living five years as having a "five-year cure." This is inaccurate: Some patients who survive five years might actually be cured, but a five-year survival rate of 50 percent means only that 50 percent of patients live for at least five years, even though many who survive five years may still have the disease and not be cured. Modern medicine is very much a matter of statistics and probabilities, and knowing how the statistics are presented is essential to understanding them.

Framing Statistics

Both doctors and patients tend to look upon the statistics more favorably than they should. Doctors, wanting to maintain hope in their patients, sometimes fudge the sur-

---

TABLE 3

Example of Survival
With and Without Treatment
(Disease X)

Years after Diagnosis	Survival	
	With Treatment	**Without Treatment**
1	90%	80%
2	80%	50%
5	15%	5%

For example, two years after they had been diagnosed with Disease X, 80% of treated patients were alive, whereas only 50% of patients with no specific treatment were alive.

---

vival figures upward. Or they might quote figures from the most favorable study they can find, while ignoring less favorable reports. They almost always point out that you have a fifty-fifty chance of doing better than the average they quote, although they seldom emphasize the fifty-fifty chance of doing worse than average. Furthermore, studies show that physicians are too optimistic in their predictions of how long their patients will live; perhaps this is wishful thinking or a reflection of their belief that they can do "better" than other physicians.

CURE MEANS total elimination of the disease, whereas survival refers to how long a person lives, with or without a cure. Physicians sometimes say "cure" when they mean "survival."

Physicians also have the ability to "frame" statistics to favor one option over another. For example, sometimes physicians paint an overly bleak picture of the outcome with no treatment, so as to encourage you to take the treatment they recommend, which may be surgery or a highly advanced technical procedure. This is another reason to ask for factual statistics about survival with—and *without*—treatment. A second opinion from another specialist in the field of your disease is a good way to get an unbiased review of the statistics.

Patients may misinterpret the statistics by hearing what they want to hear. One patient reported to me that another physician had told him he would live at least five to ten years with his newly diagnosed cancer. When I asked him to repeat what he had actually been told, after some hesitation the patient said he had been told he had an "almost 90 percent chance of living one year." He therefore figured he had a 10 percent chance of dying during the first year and the same chance of dying each year thereafter, and so he calculated a 50 percent chance of living at least five years, and a 10 percent chance of living ten years. In fact, for his disease there is a sharp cut-off in survival after one year, and fewer than half the patients survive beyond about two and a half years, even with treatment.

Discussing Options for Treatment

NEXT, DETERMINE YOUR doctor's plans for treatment. Ask her to explain in layman's terms the nature and purpose of the tests she orders, which will help her define the extent or stage of your disease. At the beginning of any serious illness that may be fatal, treatment is almost always of the "curative" type, aimed at eradicating the disease. Learn all you can about the primary curative therapy, whether it is surgery, medicines, a form of radiation therapy, or something else. Even for a disease such as AIDS, for which there is no known cure, there may be drugs or combinations of drugs that might eventually lead to a cure. For any individual patient a cure is always possible until all reasonable curative therapy has failed.

Many doctors will give you information about diagnosis and prognosis without your asking for it, or upon the least hint that you want to know it. Many physicians today believe that an informed patient will deal with the emotional or psychological aspects of a terminal illness better than an uninformed patient. They also feel that it is essential for you to know what is happening in order to deal better with the harsh treatments you must often endure. Nevertheless, if you don't ask questions, the physician will volunteer less, and you will be less informed. And no physician can know exactly what concerns you, or the things you need to know to make decisions according to your beliefs and wishes. Even if your doctor is forthcoming and clear in discussing treatment options with you, you may still want to supplement this information. If you get doctor-talk that you can't understand, which is particularly likely from a specialist, say that you don't understand the terminology and ask her to repeat the information in a different way.

Your Doctor Relationship

The beginning of your relationship with a physician sets the pattern for how the two of you will interact in the future. Like any other interpersonal relationship, it's quite difficult to change this pattern after it's established. The doctor who assumes full control over you early in your illness will expect to maintain that control later as well. On the other hand, the doctor who understands from the beginning that you want to know all you may reasonably know, and that you want to participate in decisions about your terminal illness, will keep you well involved in the later stages as well.

GETTING NO curative treatment is always an option. Ask for the survival rates with no curative therapy, and the rates with the therapy the doctor is proposing. Beware of skewed statistics.

Be aware, moreover, that you may have relationships with multiple physicians and other health care providers, and these different providers may have different styles. They may also disagree among themselves about your prognosis or the best treatment for you. Be prepared to work not just with uncertainty but with possible conflict among the people caring for you. If you sense disagreement, ask each provider politely what he thinks of the other side of the issue. You might say something such as: "Doctor, excuse me, but I'm confused because another doctor (name the doctor if appropriate) gave me a different recommendation. Is this because he's in a different specialty? Can you explain why I'm getting different opinions?"

Choosing Your Treatment(s)

THE BENEFITS OF a therapy must be balanced against any downsides it may have. Find out how a particular treatment will affect your daily living and your symptoms. Ask about complications or side effects of the proposed treatment, how long the beneficial effects will last, and how often you will have to take the treatment. How much will it cost? What will it add to survival time, on average? And, very important, ask about options. Ask about alternative treatments your doctor has available, and how they compare to what he is proposing.

One option that is always available is to choose to have no treatment, especially if the chance of a cure or remission of the disease is improbable. Ask about what you should expect with no curative therapy, or with limited treatment intended to suppress the disease without eradicating it. Ask about the survival time with no curative therapy.

Ask your doctor the following:

- What does the treatment do, and how does it work?
- How many courses of treatment will there be, and how long will each course take?
- What are the side effects of the treatment? How long until the side effects wear off?
- If surgery or a risky procedure is involved, what are possible complications? What is the risk of heart attack, stroke, or death? How long is the recovery period after surgery?
- After recovery from the treatment, what is the expected duration of remission, or the symptom-free time?
- What is the chance of a cure?
- What are the survival rates with this treatment? What are the survival rates without the treatment?

Researching Your Disease

Quite naturally, you will want to learn more about the course of your disease and how it will affect you. Some common ways of discovering more about your disease are talking to other patients with the same disease or going to a library or the Internet for written information. These sources can provide you with lots of information, some of it invaluable and, unfortunately, some of it wildly inaccurate. (See Suggested Readings for book suggestions and appendix 2 for Internet sites that might be helpful.) There are now over 15,000 Web sites on health matters, many of them with unconventional or even potentially dangerous advice, so you must be selective. Most of the mainstream sites containing information relevant to the issues discussed in this book can be found by searching under "death and dying," "cancer," or "pain."

Friends and acquaintances will offer their opinions and anecdotes, which can be helpful—and hazardous. You need to share your feelings with them and get emotional support, but unless they are medical professionals, they are unlikely to have the sort of accurate information you need. They could even misinform you, based on "knowing someone five years ago" who had the same disease. Talk to family and friends, of course, but be wary of specific information or advice based on someone else's particular condition.

Very few doctors will mind that you have gone to a library or searched online for information on your disease. In fact, they will view this as a sign of your involvement and your willingness to learn about and understand your treatments. However, physicians do worry about your outside knowledge in two ways: (1) They don't want you to make incorrect assumptions because of incomplete information or because you lack the overall knowledge and experience necessary to understand the information, and (2) they don't like you to challenge their judgment.

Challenging Your Doctor

You can avoid challenging your doctor by using non-challenging language. Instead of asking, "Why are you using drugs instead of radiation therapy?" ask your doctor to explain the advantage to you of the one over the other. If your reading leads you to wonder if a different treatment might be better, ask, "How is the treatment you propose better than . . . ?" Some patients do it very nicely by saying, "My wife (or daughter, or friend) asked me to ask you about . . . ?" If you have real concerns about the negative effects of a treatment, say so. Tell the doctor, "I have a friend who had this treatment, and it was awful," or, "I'm a little scared about this test (or treatment). Should I be?"

Learn as much as you can about the purpose and effects of your treatment so that you will be able to understand what will be happening to you and your body. This will be especially important later in the course of your illness, when you may have to decide whether to accept certain treatments that have a limited chance of success. For instance, from your readings of books, pamphlets, and on-line articles you can learn a great deal about various drugs, their side effects, and what you can expect from a specific course of chemotherapy.

TALK TO FRIENDS and family, but be wary of testimonials about treatments that may not work for you.

Although it is essential to voice any concerns and see to it that your doctor includes your input in deciding what is best for you, nevertheless, unless you want to shun medical care and "go it alone," you must trust your doctors to manage your care in the best way for you. One of the worst things about being sick is being dependent on someone else to help you, but that's the way it works in any complex business where you need expert help. Whatever you may think of doctors in general, now and to the end of your life you need a solid and mutually respectful relationship with them. You, your doctors, and your family must work together in managing your medical care.

Establishing Your Goals

After you've gotten as much information as you can from your doctor and other sources regarding your illness and the treatments for it, it's time to start thinking through your goals. Some few persons, because of age or debility or personal reasons, are ready to die shortly after learning of their terminal diagnosis, and their goals center on symptom relief or shortening the extended dying time.

But unless you feel you've already run your race, you should, initially at least, think in terms of cure, because this is almost always a possibility. Remember, a "fatal" disease can sometimes be cured. Hope for a cure is justifiable until it becomes clear that the disease is incurable, and this is never certain until all reasonable curative therapy has failed.

However, if the disease is likely to be fatal, you must now begin to assess and compare the various options available to you. You may still have months or years of good-quality life before you arrive at the final stages of dying, but you don't know for sure how long your illness will last and you need to begin planning based on your illness and condition.

Patients can have meaningful control of their potentially fatal illness through decisions about treatments that will influence how long they live, what their quality of life will be during various stages of their illness, and, in some cases, the way in which they die.

Three Categories of Treatments

You will need to choose among (1) treatments intended to cure (such as surgical removal of one entire lung, or a bone-marrow transplant), (2) treatments that have some life-prolonging effect but are primarily for decreasing unwanted symptoms (such as radiation therapy to shrink a tumor), and (3) treatments aimed entirely at relieving symptoms and with no life-prolonging effect. Keep in mind that you will want to continually review and possibly change these choices. That is, after an initial stage of therapy aimed at a cure you may eventually switch your goal to relief of symptoms and quality of life.

Often there are necessary trade-offs. Treatments aimed primarily at curing, regardless of effectiveness, sometimes necessitate a period of hellish symptoms. A bone-marrow transplant is such an example. On the other hand, an emphasis entirely on symptom control, or comfort care, may exclude the chance for a cure. The real importance of setting goals is to select the trade-offs most consistent with your goals and values.

It is rarely necessary for a patient to choose between exclusively curative and symptomatic (comfort care) therapies, until perhaps close to the end. That is, choosing therapy designed to cure does not mean you cannot also have treatment to relieve symptoms. Intermediate treatments, life-prolonging but not curative, which give added good-quality time are often available.

Changing Your Goals

Your goals may change as your illness proceeds. You may initially be willing to accept a period of increased symptoms as the cost of living long enough to see your children, or grandchildren, through school. You may later in the course of your disease become unwilling to endure the extended suffering that further curative treatment would mean for you and your family. For each proposed treatment or test, for each option along the way, you will have to choose according to the goal that seems best at the time.

While you are still in the early stage of your illness it may seem unnecessary to think things through all the way to the end. But planning only a bit at a time and waiting until a change in your illness forces a new round of decisions doesn't let you set the overall best course into and through the process of dying. Even now, when you have months or years of good-quality life remaining, you must become familiar with the problems that may arise in later stages of your illness, and you need to begin setting goals.

UNLESS YOU FEEL that because of age or debility you should allow your life to come to an end, your first goal should be a cure.

The goal of many who reach the terminal phase of their illness—after curative therapy has failed—is minimizing suffering during the late dying phase. There are three strategies for achieving this goal:

1. Minimize the extended dying period
2. Maximize comfort care, and, for some few
3. Directly shorten the dying period through aid-in-dying

We will discuss these strategies more extensively in later chapters.

Summary

1. Find out the diagnosis—what the disease is and how it alters the structure and functioning of your body.

2. Ask about the prognosis, which is the forecast of the course of the disease.

3. Understand the difference between cure, which means total elimination or eradication of the disease, and survival, which means how long a person lives, with or without a cure.

4. Learn how physicians use statistics to predict survival.

5. Learn everything you can about the treatment your doctor proposes for you. Ask about side effects, how the treatment will affect your daily living, and what it will add to survival time. Compare survival time with and without treatment. Compare the proposed treatment with other treatment options.

6. Be wary of testimonials from family and friends about treatments that worked for some patients but may not be good for you.

7. In non-challenging ways, discuss with your doctors any questions or concerns you have about what the best treatment is for you.

8. Develop a team approach, with you, your doctors, and your family learning about your condition and making treatment decisions together.

9. Set your goals for treatment based on your life situation and condition. For most patients who have just learned of having a potentially fatal disease, a cure is possible and maximal curative therapy is initially the best goal.

10. Be ready to change your goals if your illness worsens and cure becomes unlikely.

· 7 ·

Planning in the World of Curative Therapy

Doctors are engaged in an almost spiritual battle against disease. To the physician, death is the enemy, an evil, and the working premise of modern medicine is to use all means of combating it, which means using all available curative therapies. Physicians treat patients primarily by attempting to eradicate diseases rather than relieve symptoms. This is particularly true when biophysical abnormalities threaten the patient with death.

At first glance this goal may seem obvious and appropriate, but this deeply embedded professional imperative to cure can drive doctors to give medical care that is inappropriate for peaceful dying. For example, if a patient is dying because of a weak heart and is having chest pains, his doctors may choose to do open heart surgery to "fix" the clogged arteries in his heart—even though they know there is almost no reasonable hope for improvement of his severely damaged heart. This "do everything possible" approach carries a large risk of going through the distress of major surgery with little or no benefit, or premature death at the time of surgery.

In this chapter we will explore how the routine use of curative treatment can control the way you die if you do not maintain some control over your medical treatments.

How Physicians Treat Patients: A Cascading Application of Technologies

TODAY PHYSICIANS HELP their patients by focusing on the technology that works so well and has delivered the promise of longer and better life. Medical technology does save lives and extend meaningful life, but later in the course of some illnesses its application can lead to a new and harder-to-cure condition, for which we seek yet another technological treatment. This cascading application of technologies has a clinical momentum almost impossible to stop, which can lead to a situation that is not in the best interest of the patient.

Prolonging Life at All Costs

The presumption is always to try to cure, or at least to prolong life, and for physicians it is professionally suspect or wrong not to do so. For example, if two or more physicians disagree on the advisability of using yet another curative treatment even when both agree the outlook is probably hopeless, the activist who wants to use the treatment almost always prevails. The burden of proof is always on the one who says not to try. Among physicians, to miss a chance to cure is a greater professional sin than to cause harm or extend suffering in a brave attempt to cure.

I recently observed a patient, Bob K., who, after four years of multiple hospitalizations and escalating treatment for end-stage congestive heart failure and kidney failure, was again in the hospital, where all attempts to improve his condition with intravenous drugs were for naught. Bob knew he would soon die and asked to go home. The consultants, mainstream physicians, countered by ordering kidney dialysis and a balloon pump to assist his failing heart. Not to "give him every chance," they said, was "unethical." In the name of "good medicine," or the professional "standard of care," they prolonged their patient's dying ordeal by about two weeks and deprived Bob of his wish to die at home. In this case, which is not uncommon or unusual, the physicians' drive to cure entirely overshadowed considerations of symptom relief and the desires of the patient.

Furthermore, the medical culture discourages noncurative attention to dying patients. This is observable in virtually all major hospitals. When a patient teeters on the edge of death but is considered salvageable, the patient's hospital room is often full to frenetic capacity with machines, nurses, consultants, medical residents and students, and therapists of all sorts. But when every last attempt to cure has failed and the morphine drip has been started, no one enters the room for hours at a time. When a physician says to the family, "There's nothing more to do," it means that everything possible has been done in an attempt to cure, and nothing can save the patient. When a cure is no longer possible the physician often withdraws. To physicians this is not abandonment but a statement of their inability to cure and therefore the end of their role in care of the patient.

Fortunately, increasing numbers of physicians today, even many specialists who use leading-edge technology, do not abandon their dying patients and do understand the limitations of technology when it is of little or no benefit. They recognize that even when a patient is near death there is always something more they can do—namely, give better comfort care and relief from symptoms. But even in today's improved environment, with the new emphasis on comfort care, the prevalent and often overwhelming medical practice of using every curative therapy available, of "doing everything possible," is difficult for any physician, and therefore any patient, to avoid.

> MEDICAL technology has a clinical momentum almost impossible to stop.

Futile Therapy

Physicians sometimes speak of futile therapy. By this they mean a technology—such as chemotherapy or an operation—that is unlikely to achieve its medical purpose. Whether a treatment is futile for you depends on your goals. For someone young and dying of cancer, a treatment with a five percent chance of cure may not be futile.

The same treatment, with the same chance of cure, would be futile for an older person whose goal is palliative care. As you approach the need to make difficult end-of-life medical decisions, keep in mind that some technological therapy is always available for doctors to use for any condition, but if it is futile in terms of your goals, it can cause harm or increased suffering.

A lot of patients receive futile therapy at the end of life. You may too unless you have a clear understanding with your physicians in advance about when to stop attempts to prolong your life.

Choosing Your Primary Decision-Making Doctor

A GOOD WAY to begin decision making is to choose the doctor with whom you want to work most closely in making end-of-life decisions. This is often not easy, as very early in the course of your illness, possibly even before the diagnosis is established, you may see experts who are more knowledgeable about your specific disease than is your primary doctor, and these experts may assume the primary direction of your care. You may see a multitude of specialists, and maybe your care will be directed by a committee of physicians. Frequently the curative therapy you receive (including the side effects of it) is so important that the specialist administering it is the best person to coordinate your overall care. If you have cancer, your oncologist often becomes the primary doctor. And, of course, if you have surgery, the surgeon must be in charge, at least until recovery from the surgery. But specialists are always working together with other doctors.

There need be no problem in working closely with two or more doctors, and some patients do it well. But for many it works best to identify one doctor with whom you will make important end-of-life decisions. You need at least one physician who understands you and your needs, and on whom you can lean. If you choose your primary-care physician as your ultimate spokesperson, tell her of your wish to have her involved in all important decisions, and that you will tell all specialists they must clear in advance all major decisions with her. Even if the primary doctor wishes to defer most medical decisions to specialists, asking her to remain involved in decision making has the major advantage of keeping her informed and ready to resume direction of your case if and when curative therapy fails and the experts back away from you.

Go over your advance directives with each doctor who may participate in major decisions. Even if you reviewed your living will and durable power of attorney just months ago, do it again now that you know your diagnosis. Be sure copies are in all your medical records.

Expectations and Hard Reality

FOR MANY IF not most patients, especially younger ones, the choice of the treatment with the best chance of cure is obviously correct. This is the default position. Nevertheless, you must assess all information fully and try to be realistic about treatment outcomes. One medical study found that 82 percent of patients with late-stage lung cancer or widely spread colon cancer had unrealistic and overoptimistic beliefs about their long-term chances.[1]

Compared to the more realistic patients, the overly optimistic patients were more likely to choose aggressive and futile curative treatments, were more often readmitted to hospitals during the course of treatments, and were more likely to die on a mechanical respirator. Sadly, the study showed that when compared to similar patients who chose to forgo aggressive curative treatments, the overly optimistic patients had a worse quality of life and did not live any longer. This cold, hard fact is worth remembering.

Even physicians who understand the frequent futility of curative therapy find it difficult not to yield to the plea of a dying patient for "one more chance." I am sad to say, I have watched many terminally ill patients "go for the cure" only to end up more incapacitated after "the cure" than before. Whether to try a potentially dangerous curative treatment is perhaps the most excruciatingly difficult decision that patients need to make, and I have watched even terminally ill physicians—as patients—agonize over the best course.

REALISTIC planning is not inconsistent with hope.

A physician friend, sixty-eight years old, developed a rare form of leukemia. After two courses of chemothera-

---

1. Jane C. Weeks et al., *Journal of the American Medical Association,* "Relationship between Cancer Patients' Predictions of Prognosis and Their Treatment Preferences." June 3, 1998, vol. 279, pp. 1709–17.

py, his doctors suggested a bone-marrow transplant. For his particular disease and condition, a cure was a long shot, and he knew it. Nevertheless, he told me, "I think the treatment is better than they say, so I'm going for it." After going through the ordeal of massive chemotherapy and radiation therapy, his transplant was not successful and he died four weeks later.

My advice is not to shrink from a factual assessment of the probable outcome of any choice you are considering.

Fight for Survival but Prepare for Dying

Once you have absorbed the shock of having a potentially fatal illness and have settled on a medical plan for treating it, talking realistically to your doctor about the possibility or eventuality of medical failure is a good idea because it alerts your doctor to your unwillingness to accept futile treatment. This is not to say you must proceed as though you surely will die soon from your disease and therefore should not "fight" it. Fight to your fullest, abso-lutely, for this is what gives you the best chance of survival.

Preparation for dying does not undermine your fight for survival any more than making out your will and advance directives did years earlier. To use the classical fighting analogy, a general who leads his army into a great battle without any plan for retreat is an unwise general. Preparation is a precaution and is not inconsistent with hope. Use hope to support yourself through the rigors of treatment, but don't let blind hope lead you willy-nilly to worthless or even quack therapies, or deter you from doing the necessary work of planning for the end. Some patients are within weeks or days of dying when they and their doctors realize there is nothing more to gain from curative therapy. Waiting until that point in your process may leave insufficient time for effective planning.

Unconventional or Alternative Therapies

Many patients with potentially fatal illnesses seek unconventional therapies in hope of a cure. Most alternative therapies are not as harsh as chemotherapy or surgery, but, if you want to avoid futile treatments, you must be equally realistic in determining accurate survival or cure rates for any type of treatment you choose.

If you are interested in alternative medicine options—e.g., chiropractic, acupuncture, or natural remedies that conventional doctors don't give and may not approve of—tell your doctors. They need to know because it could affect what they are doing. Most mainstream physicians will not mind your seeking alternative treatments unless they interfere with your conventional treatments. For instance, if you should travel to a foreign country for a "cure" you would most likely be unable to continue or keep on schedule with your regular medical treatments. Also, some alternative medicines or diets may interfere with or impede the action of the conventional drugs you are taking. Doctors need to plan your course, so they need to know if you have ideas for other treatments.

Summary

1. Understand how physicians use curative therapy and that futile therapy may prolong your dying process.

2. Choose a trusted doctor who will be your spokes-person for major medical decisions, but let all your doctors know your treatment goals.

3. Guard against overoptimistic interpretation of statistics or your ability to "beat the odds."

4. Maintain your hope, but be realistic about probabilities for a cure.

5. If you choose an alternative or unconventional treatment, tell your regular doctor.

· 8 ·

The Options
of Assisted Dying

IN THIS CHAPTER we will discuss the options of assisted dying, also known as physician *aid-in-dying*. The term "aid-in-dying" refers to any means of hastening death, or shortening the dying process, that requires or involves the help of a physician or other medical provider. For example, a request not to be resuscitated in a medical facility is a request for an indirect form of aid-in-dying, because the patient requires the agreement and cooperation of her physicians to achieve what she wants. The direct forms of aid-in-dying that we will discuss include (1) withdrawal of life-supporting or life-prolonging therapy, (2) aggressive comfort care that may possibly alter the time of dying, and (3) physician-assisted suicide. If you think you will want any of these options, you must discuss them with your physicians, at least those you trust, so that when the time comes, they will be able to help you achieve your wishes.

Dying is a medically managed process for virtually all patients who receive medical care at the end of life, and you should be familiar with specific methods of physician aid-in-dying. These methods include

- Refusing resuscitation
- Refusing or withdrawing life-sustaining therapy
- Fasting (starvation) with symptom control
- Terminal sedation (fasting with sedation)
- Physician-assisted suicide

Legal Methods of Assisted Dying

IN ADDITION TO providing aggressive comfort care for relief of distressful symptoms, physicians can do—or avoid doing—several things to shorten the dying process.

Refusing Resuscitation

As we discussed in chapter 2, resuscitation (often called CPR for "cardio-pulmonary resuscitation") refers to procedures done to restart the heart and breathing when they have ceased to function effectively after cardiac arrest.

Many patients are resuscitated from cardiac arrest at the time of a heart attack or stroke or during surgery and recover fully to the condition they were in prior to cardiac arrest. When the condition they are restored to is one of normal or reasonable health, the procedure leads to a continuation of a good or meaningful life. However, resuscitation also is applied to patients whose hearts stop at the end of their dying process, returning them to the condition they were in prior to cardiac arrest, or worse.

The advisability of having CPR therefore hinges on the benefit of staying alive. If a patient is terminally ill, has lost almost all bodily function, and is suffering, it's hard to understand how CPR could be a benefit. The medical history of the past twenty-five years is sadly replete with examples of terminally ill patients with no hope for recovery who have been resuscitated to endure days or weeks of more agony before dying.

The Do Not Resuscitate Directive

Therefore, if you have a terminal illness, you must decide when or under what conditions you desire resuscitation. At one extreme, you can request resuscitation under any or all conditions, with the understanding, of course, that doctors have no obligation to resuscitate a patient repeatedly if cardiac arrest recurs shortly after each resuscitation. At the other extreme, you may request "do not resuscitate" (DNR) under any circumstances. This is entirely legal and ethical. Anyone age 18 or older may refuse any form of medical treatment, and resuscitation is a treatment. Furthermore, you need not be terminally ill (defined as a prognosis of less than six months to live) to sign a DNR order, which you may include in your living will and durable power of attorney. In many states you can obtain from the state health department an official DNR directive to carry with you in case you have a cardiac arrest outside a medical facility, where medical personnel called to resuscitate you would not otherwise know about your DNR directive.

Inappropriate Resuscitations

One of the more sickening scenes one can experience in a hospital is that of a patient who has just gained final peace and release from a long-endured terminal illness of emaciation and suffering. At the moment of cardiac arrest, an alarm goes off at the central monitoring station, and someone present, perhaps a clerk who may never have talked to the patient, pushes the button for a "code," or resuscitation. The "code" team, often swelled to more than ten people by other medical personnel on-site, arrives and pushes into the room with the paraphernalia of resuscitation. After resuscitation, the family arrives to see their loved one unable to speak and perhaps even unable to respond, but still alive. If the patient is fortunate, he is unaware of any sensation, but for the family it may be a moment of unpardonable and irreconcilable grief.

RESUSCITATION brings wonderful benefits when it serves to prolong meaningful life, but for patients who have reached the end of the dying process it can give unwanted extension of suffering.

Inappropriate resuscitations, although common in hospitals just ten years ago, are now mercifully less common because physicians, and especially nurses, are attentive to the possibility and speak to patients and/or their families about DNR orders in the last stages of dying. Hospitals and other medical facilities are obligated by law to have someone ask patients their preferences about DNR at the time of admission. Many patients and family members do not want to talk about DNR, and some vigorously object to any mention of the subject, but if you are going to direct your process of dying you must understand how important this issue is, whatever your decision on it is. Be aware that to ignore or deny the question of DNR is to choose to be resuscitated.

Putting DNR in Your Medical Record

If your goal is to avoid futile resuscitation, you need a DNR order. This is possible through your advance directive, or by your request at any time when in a medical institution. Remind the staff of your wishes every time you enter a hospital or any sort of health care facility. All you need do is tell the doctor or the nurse, "I request no resuscitation." They may ask you to sign a form, and they will note it conspicuously in your medical record. You may change your mind and your DNR directive at any time.

Refusing Life-Sustaining Treatment

When you are in the early stages of a terminal illness you most likely will be getting curative or life-prolonging therapy and will not be dependent on treatments or life-support measures just to stay alive. When near to the end, however, most patients who are dying slowly are on some form of treatment that is sustaining life, such as a pacemaker, kidney dialysis, or an essential medicine.

By definition, if someone removes or withdraws a treatment necessary for survival, such as a respirator (ventilator), or a feeding tube in someone unable to eat, the patient will die. Any patient has the legal right to refuse or withdraw any treatment, including those that could or are sustaining life. In order to withdraw life-sustaining treatment, the desire of a patient who is not capable of making medical decisions must be clear in advance directives or other statements.

Stopping Medicines That Prolong Dying

As we discussed in chapter 2, the best-known form of withdrawal of life-sustaining treatment is to disconnect a patient from a ventilator. The most common form of withdrawal of life-sustaining treatment in terms of frequency is simply the stopping of intravenous medicines. In hospitals or nursing facilities, it is very common practice to stop all medicines for patients who are on the brink of dying after all curative therapy has failed and when it has become clear to everyone that further treatment will only delay dying and therefore prolong suffering. In the usual situation the patient is in shock or nearly in shock, and blood pressure is being kept up to survival levels by intravenous drugs and fluids or blood transfusions. With continuing treatment this might go on for days or even weeks, but when these treatments are stopped, blood pressure falls and the patient usually dies within hours.

Dialysis, Pacemakers, and Defibrillators

In most instances, physicians and nurses are fully involved in the actual stopping of any therapy that keeps a patient alive because they must take steps to stop it. One instance in which they may not be directly involved is in the cessation of kidney dialysis. The average patient who has lost effective kidney function requires dialysis three times a week; otherwise death follows in about a week. This is usually a painless, peaceful dying, as the patient slowly sinks into a coma and dies from the buildup of toxic substances in the blood. The act of refusing to continue kidney dialysis is not suicide; it is the voluntary withdrawal of a life-sustaining treatment.

MOST PATIENTS who are dying slowly are on some form of treatment that is prolonging the process. Withholding or withdrawing this treatment is the most common form of physician aid-in-dying.

In a similar manner, patients who are dependent on implanted pacemakers or defibrillators may request to have them turned off, although this is not possible for some types of pacemakers. Naturally enough, such instruments are designed so they cannot be turned off accidentally and so must be turned off by a physician or a technician. I had a patient—Jonas—who had had an implanted defibrillator for three years when he developed an increasingly weak heart and had great difficulty breathing. Jonas was in a terminal condition, too weak to sit up by himself and constantly short of breath. Because of increased episodes of ventricular fibrillation (a form of cardiac arrest), his implanted defibrillator shocked his heart (automatic CPR) about once every two or three days, each time staving off natural death by giving painful jolts to his chest with each shock. Jonas requested that I turn off the defibrillator, which I did, and he died quietly and peacefully two days later, at home with his family. This is a passive form of aid-in-dying, but it requires the assistance of a physician to implement.

Blood Transfusions and Steroid Drugs

Many patients need periodic blood transfusions, without which they would die quickly. Some patients are dependent on specific drugs, without which they would die in hours or days. Steroids, or drugs resembling cortisone, are necessary for some patients to prevent collapse of blood pressure or to prevent fatal swelling of the brain. Other patients are dependent on drugs to prevent heart fibrillation or cardiac arrest. Withdrawing a drug that is essential for sustaining life may not result in a quick death, but, depending on the drug and the patient's physical condition, may result in death in a matter of days.

Feeding Tubes

Withdrawing a feeding tube from a patient otherwise unable to eat is another form of withdrawal of life-sustaining treatment. Initially some physicians and medical ethicists had doubts about this practice, because they viewed the administration of food and water as essential, natural care, not medical treatment. Ultimately the courts, including the U.S. Supreme Court, found that administration of food and liquids through artificial means such as a feeding tube constituted treatment that a patient could refuse.

Withdrawal of life-sustaining treatment in any of its myriad forms is a means of shortening the dying process. Be aware of these options and the treatments you are receiving, and tell your physician if you want to have the option of withdrawing essential or life-sustaining therapy, if necessary and if possible. Almost all physicians are comfortable with this form of assisted dying; they consider it "natural" dying. It is, after all, just stopping the unnatural medical prolongation of the dying process.

Fasting (Starvation)

No patient need take nourishment or fluids against her wishes. This is true also when the patient is dependent on feeding through a feeding tube or intravenous lines. Therefore, fasting is a legal option open to any dying patient, and a considerable number of dying patients who wish to die peacefully do literally and purposefully fast to death. Although some people consider fasting a form of suicide, most people—including most physicians—view it as an acceptable form of refusing life-sustaining therapy. It is not suicide in the ordinary sense. Be advised that medical providers commonly refer to terminal fasting as "starvation," and if you use the term "fasting" they may not understand you.

The length of the fast can vary depending on how nourished or wasted the patient is at the start of fasting. A person on the very brink of death who is being sustained by intravenous fluids and nourishment might die a day or two after all intravenous feeding is stopped. A dying person who has been eating reasonably well might live

FASTING (starvation) is an option open to any dying patient.

three weeks after all feeding is stopped. The average terminal fast is seven to fourteen days.

For many terminally ill persons, fasting leads to somnolence and progressively longer periods of unresponsiveness until death, while other patients remain clear-minded almost to the end. Although fasting can lead to a good death for some, it is usually a slow process and most patients do complain of thirst while lingering for what may seem to family and friends an interminable time. In most cases small sips of water or ice chips in the mouth can alleviate thirst.

Most patients for whom observers report a good dying process have received morphine or a sedative for control of discomfort during their fasting. If you think you may become interested in this option, understand that in most cases it is necessary to receive supplemental drugs such as morphine to control or relieve symptoms that develop during the fast.

A physician friend's father was dying and told his son to "get it over with." His son said he was unwilling to give him a lethal medicine, but told his father that he would keep him very comfortable if he stopped eating and drinking. This was arranged, and every time the father said he had any thirst or hunger the nurse gave him enough morphine to eliminate the distress. Within four days the father slipped into a coma, and he died two days after that. It was a peaceful death.

Terminal Sedation

With the help of your doctor, you can carry fasting a step further with terminal sedation. Continuous sedation to unconsciousness gives the ultimate relief of symptoms during fasting. This method is seldom necessary, but for a terminally ill and suffering patient it is legal and is considered ethical by most of the medical profession.

In practice, terminal sedation with a barbiturate to produce unconsciousness is nearly the same as the practice of using sufficient morphine to minimize or eliminate symptoms during fasting; both are forms of aggressive comfort care. As a practical matter, when death appears to be hours or at most a few days away physicians most commonly use high doses of morphine, which is very effective in suppressing awareness of symptoms during withdrawal of fluids and nutrition. However, when morphine is used in doses high enough to induce unconsciousness there is often a technical problem of tolerance to the drug, which over time may allow intermittent consciousness. When death appears to be many days or weeks away, and continuous unconsciousness is the only means of relieving symptoms, terminal sedation with barbiturates can more effectively produce continuous unconsciousness than is usually possible with intravenous morphine.

Although most physicians consider terminal sedation to be ethical, others consider it a relatively active method of hastening or causing death. These physicians may refuse to administer barbiturates, yet they may be willing to use morphine and other sedatives on an "as needed" or continuous basis to suppress awareness of symptoms.

The names given to these procedures are exceedingly important to physicians involved in the practices, as they define both how physicians feel about what they are doing and public perception of the practices. It is necessary for you to understand your physician's position and sensitivity on these issues and to use language appropriate to your physician's needs, although you yourself may not find these semantic distinctions meaningful. In general, if a dying patient asks for sedation not as a means to die, but as a form of comfort care, most physicians will honor the request.

IN MY OPINION, cessation of all therapy and total starvation (including no fluids) is a reasonable option for relieving suffering at the end of life as long as you are assured of getting sufficient symptomatic relief with painkillers and/or sedatives during the starvation period. Also, it is important that your family and friends understand the process and realize that it may go on a week or two—possibly longer. Continuous sedation with a barbiturate is a means by which any patient can obtain complete and lasting relief of symptoms at the cost of unconsciousness from the beginning of the treatment to the end. If you desire this option if it should become necessary, you should discuss it with your doctor well in advance, to determine his willingness to work with you throughout the time it takes.

Physician-Assisted Suicide

PHYSICIAN-ASSISTED SUICIDE, whether we like it or not, is an option available to many dying patients. It is chosen by a few patients and desired by many as a fallback option. Most people are aware of this practice through media attention to attempts to legalize it. Oregon is the only state where it is currently legal. Although it is illegal in other states, it nevertheless occurs, and the majority of physicians and adults in this country believe dying patients should have access to some form of assisted dying, within guidelines to prevent abuse. Realistically, physician-assisted suicide is an option many people think about and consider, although it is rarely necessary to prevent physical suffering. As you enter the stage of terminal illness it is appropriate to discuss this most controversial issue well in advance of the time you might seek to use it.

What Physician-Assisted Suicide Is and Is Not

By definition, physician-assisted suicide occurs when a physician provides the means with which a patient voluntarily ends his life. With assisted suicide, as opposed to euthanasia, the physician does not administer a lethal medicine or directly cause the death of the patient but assists by writing a prescription for the drugs. The act itself, the administering of the lethal drugs, is performed voluntarily by the patient.

If a doctor actually administers a lethal dose of pills, as through a feeding tube or by injecting a lethal medicine, the act is considered *voluntary euthanasia* if the patient is competent and requests it. If the patient is not competent to make medical decisions or does not voluntarily request it, the act is considered to be *involuntary euthanasia*. Both types of euthanasia are illegal in the United States.

If a person voluntarily asks for pills and ends her life by taking them herself, and if the physician has prescribed the pills for the purpose of ending the person's life, the act is physician-assisted suicide. However, if a patient ends her life with lethal pills that the physician has prescribed for a purpose other than ending life, e.g., for pain relief or sleep, it is not physician-assisted suicide.

In physician-assisted suicide, as well as in terminal sedation or withdrawal of life-sustaining therapy, the motive of the physician is to stop suffering, and the end result is the same—death of the patient. However, the distinctions between the practices are important for many people. We justify terminal sedation by saying that the patient dies

> **PHYSICIAN-** assisted suicide— illegal in all states except Oregon— occurs when a physician provides or prescribes the lethal drugs but does not administer them.

"naturally" by refusing fluids and nutrition, that the physician's act of administering a drug sedates the patient but does not directly kill her. When a patient dies relatively quickly after ingestion of lethal drugs obtained from a physician, even though the physician's intent may be to end suffering and not to end life, we say the physician has assisted in suicide. This raises profound moral and legal issues over the appropriate role of physicians and what practices our society is willing to accept as public policy.

The debate rages as to whether dying by ingestion of drugs prescribed by a physician is suicide when performed by someone who is terminally ill. Supporters call it rational or preemptive suicide, arguing that it is not suicide in the ordinary sense. Those who oppose any legal form of the practice insist on calling it suicide and attach to it the stigma and legal prohibition of ordinary suicide.

The incidence of physician-assisted suicide in the United States is unknown because the practice is legal and reported only in the state of Oregon. Furthermore, there is room for considerable ambiguity in defining the act. Many patients obtain lethal drugs to end their lives if necessary later in their dying process, but never use the drugs for that purpose. In other words, many patients have assisted suicide as a "fallback" option but for a variety of reasons never use it.

Making Physician-Assisted Suicide an Option

To succeed in dying with prescription pills, a patient must obtain the necessary amount of drugs. Some patients achieve this directly through one physician, some by obtaining prescriptions from multiple physicians. In a study from Washington State, physicians gave prescriptions to 24 percent of the terminally ill patients who requested drugs for ending life.[1]

Other patients obtain the drugs from friends or through networks such as those that are said to exist for patients with AIDS.

Some patients obtain drugs from physicians who are willing to write prescriptions for these drugs to be used as sedatives (for sleep) or symptom relief, but not for the stated purpose of ending life. Being present with a patient who takes a lethal dose of pills would be incriminating for a physician if she were prosecuted under state assisted-suicide laws. Therefore, many physicians who are willing to write prescriptions to put lethal pills in the hands of their patients are not willing to be present when the patient takes them.

If you want the option of physician-assisted suicide, you should mention this to your physician, but use caution. In broaching this subject with your doctor you may well change your relationship with her. If she is sympathetic, your relationship will probably become closer and more intimate as you discuss your goals and hopes. If your doctor is unsympathetic to this approach to dying, she may become more distant, emotionally and professionally. If you stay with a doctor who is unsympathetic to your

---

1. Anthony L. Back, Jeffrey I. Wallace, Helene E. Starks, Robert A. Perlman, "Physician-Assisted Suicide and Euthanasia in Washington State," *Journal of the American Medical Association*, March 27, 1996, vol. 275, pp. 919–925.

desire for the option of physician-assisted suicide, the strain on your relationship may be detrimental to your overall medical care. She might, for example, under-prescribe painkillers out of concern that you may use them to end your life. This physician may also speak to your relatives in an attempt to dissuade you from your desire or even have you moved to a facility where you could not carry out assisted suicide.

Euthanasia

If you mention euthanasia you risk rupturing your relationship with your doctor. In physician-assisted suicide, you give yourself the drugs, while in euthanasia the doctor must directly perform the act. This is a very large difference, given our laws, social attitudes, and professional standards. Although some physicians do perform euthanasia when asked by a suffering patient in the final throes of dying, physicians in the United States are much more reluctant to perform euthanasia than to be involved directly or indirectly in physician-assisted suicide. Even those physicians willing to perform euthanasia as a rare exception would not want to commit to it in advance. If your concern is having to endure great pain or suffering at the end of

EVEN THOSE physicians willing to perform euthanasia as a rare exception would not want to commit to it in advance.

life, remember that more and more physicians today are willing to give enough comfort care with a narcotic or sedative to eliminate a dying patient's distress.

Preemptive Assisted Suicide

All physician-assisted suicides are preemptive in the sense that they hasten the end of a patient's life by days, weeks, or months before it otherwise would end. But some patients who have an incurable or ultimately fatal illness seek to end life before they enter the final stage of debility, dependency, and disintegration of body. They may fear that if they wait too long they will lose the ability to control their destiny by becoming physically unable to swallow the pills. Patients with Lou Gehrig's disease, for example, ultimately become unable to swallow, as well as losing muscle control over breathing and bowel and bladder function. Once a patient has reached this phase of the disease she is no longer able to end her life by taking pills.

However, someone who has an incurable disease but is not terminally ill may live a relatively long time—perhaps even years. What does a physician with a patient with Lou Gehrig's disease do in deciding the degree of preemptiveness she can accept?

An assisted suicide of such a person is outside the limits even of mainstream proposals for legalized physician-assisted suicide, one of which is that it should be allowed only for patients who have less than six months to live. In Oregon, for instance, where physician-assisted suicide is legal under given criteria, it is illegal for a physician to assist in the suicide of someone who has a probable survival of more than six months, regardless of that patient's incurable condition or suffering.

Therefore, realize that even among sympathetic physicians, very few are willing to assist in dying anyone who has not entered the phase of terminal illness with less than six months to live. However, it does happen.

The Legal Status of Physician-Assisted Suicide

Where does all this leave you, the patient, if you are interested in the option of physician-assisted suicide? The composite of state statutes and court opinions, including two cases decided by the U.S. Supreme Court, upholds the legal ban for now, except in the state of Oregon. Although physician-assisted suicide is illegal, suicide is not, and you, the patient are not committing an illegal act if you take a lethal dose of drugs.

Although physician-assisted suicide is not legal, the majority of the public and physicians believe doctors should be allowed to painlessly end a dying patient's life if the patient and family request it.[2]

Furthermore, many persons who oppose legalized physician-assisted suicide wish to reserve it as a private option for themselves or for others who need it. For example, more physicians than are willing to assist their patients

---

2. Charles McKhann, *A Time to Die,* Yale University Press, New Haven, 1999, p. 88; Institute of Medicine, *Approaching Death,* National Academy Press, Washington, D.C. 1997, p. 45.

in this manner want the option of physician-assisted suicide for themselves. In fact, physicians constitute a group of citizens who are uniquely able to obtain drugs, and more than any other group in our society they may avail themselves of the option of assisted suicide in privacy.

Many physicians who are staunch opponents of legalized physician-assisted suicide will admit to knowing heart-wrenching cases in which they agree that the patient would be best served by being helped to die. The author and surgeon Sherwin Nuland wrote: "If the fully informed person whose suffering I cannot relieve repeatedly asks that I aid him in his determination to end his life, whether by pill or injection, I am obligated to do so. A tolerant society should allow it."[3]

> **EVEN MANY OF those who are against legalizing it believe physician-assisted suicide should be allowable as a private act.**

Dr. Nuland does not favor legalized physician-assisted suicide, but he defends the rare occasion when a physician helps a patient die as being consistent with the higher ideal of the Hippocratic oath of acting for "the benefit of the sick." Dr. Nuland, like many physicians, makes a distinction between public policy and private medical acts.

Members of the legal profession also have expressed objection to legalization of physician-assisted suicide even

---

3. Sherwin B. Nuland, "Doctors, Patients, and the End: The Right to Live," *The New Republic,* Nov. 2, 1998, pp. 29–35.

while wanting to have the option available for themselves or those who need it. In the last sentence of an article outlining his opposition to legalizing physician-assisted suicide, a noted lawyer wrote: "At the same time I selfishly reserve my right to do in private what my family, my doctor and pastor and I, in loving consultation, voluntarily agree is best."[4]

How the contradiction between public policy and private acts of dying will work out in the years ahead is unknown, but for now you must plan within the ambiguity of the law and physicians' practices enshrouding this issue. For now, physician-assisted suicide remains a private matter.

If you are interested in assisted suicide, you should think about when in the course of your dying process you want to use this option and begin discussions with your doctor, family, and other trusted advisors. Above all, keep in mind, this is not something to go into lightly. It is an ultimate step with enduring consequences to many besides yourself. It is usually not necessary because there are other options to relieve pain and even consciousness, as discussed already. Go cautiously and carefully, and not alone.

---

4. John H. Pickering, "The Continuing Debate over Active Euthanasia," *Bioethics Bulletin,* American Bar Association, Summer 1994, vol. 3, no. 2. pp. 1–15.

Summary

Legal Methods of Assisted Dying

1. You must decide when or under what conditions you desire resuscitation and tell your doctors your desires.

2. To ignore or to deny the question of DNR is to choose to be resuscitated.

3. You may change your mind and your DNR directive at any time.

4. Every time you enter a hospital or any sort of health care facility, remind the staff of your directive for or not for DNR.

5. Become familiar with the purposes and mechanisms of all drugs and other treatments you may receive, and find out whether any are life-sustaining.

6. The withdrawal of any drug, instrument, or treatment that is keeping a patient alive will shorten the dying process and is a form of physician aid-in-dying.

7. Fasting (starvation) is an effective method of shortening the dying process, but patients may linger days to weeks. In most cases morphine or a similar drug is necessary to control thirst and hunger or other symptoms present during fasting.

8. If morphine is not sufficient to suppress symptoms, and dying appears to be days or weeks away, barbiturates

can induce continuous unconsciousness and elimination of all suffering.

9. If you desire the option of fasting, with or without terminal sedation, you should discuss it with your doctor well in advance.

Physician-Assisted Suicide

1. Physician-assisted suicide is used by a small number of dying patients but is sought as an available option by many more who ultimately never need or use it.

2. If you are interested in the option of assisted suicide, discuss it with your physician. Physicians are most reluctant to participate in helping patients die who do not have less than six months to live.

3. It is not illegal for you to take lethal drugs, but it is illegal for a physician to prescribe lethal drugs for the purpose of ending life, except in the state of Oregon.

4. If you end your life with lethal drugs prescribed by a physician for medical purposes other than to end life, it is not physician-assisted suicide and the physician has not acted illegally.

5. It is a social paradox that many persons who oppose assisted suicide as public policy wish to have the option for themselves. It remains a private matter.

6. Assisted suicide is usually not necessary because there are other options to relieve pain and induce unconsciousness.

· 9 ·

Getting Found

TELLING CLOSE FRIENDS and family about your diagnosis can be extremely difficult. You may feel like hiding instead. However, although you are the one with the fatal illness, it is not just you who will be deeply involved in and affected by your illness. "No man is an island," as the poet John Donne pointed out. No matter who you are, there are persons out there—in most cases a lot of them—who will be profoundly affected by what is happening to you.

In his book *All I Need to Know I Learned in Kindergarten*, Robert Fulghum tells a story about the game of hide-and-seek. A group of kids often played the game, and there was always one kid who hid so well that the others couldn't find him. In fact, it ruined things, as the other kids could never finish a game because they couldn't find the kid who hid so well. Every time they played they ended up mad at this kid, and finally they had to tell him he couldn't play with them.

After telling this story, Fulghum then tells about a man who developed cancer. Out of a desire not to "bother"

other people with his problem, he withdrew more and more as he grew sicker, confiding in no one. And then he suddenly died. When his friends and co-workers found out what had happened, they were mortified at what they perceived to be their own failure to help him during his dying days. They felt guilty that they hadn't had the ability to see his distress and to comfort him in his last days. Also, they were angry he hadn't had the interest, respect, or civility to share his problem with them. They were upset with him—mad at him—with no means of coming to terms with their distress. It was not a good game. He had hidden too well from them.

You will hurt those you know best if you hide when you acquire a potentially fatal illness. Like the kid in Fulghum's story, if you don't want to ruin the game, you need to "get found." Your family will have important work to do for themselves as well as for you. They need to find you.

The most compelling reason for talking with your family is that you will be better off. It's very simple—your ability to direct your dying process, if that is what you desire, will be dependent on and greatly enhanced by your family. You can't do it by yourself, without them. And they can't help you plan if you don't confide in them. So talk to them, for your own sake.

Expanding Your Family

YOUR FAMILY—THE people who mean the most to you, and to whom you mean the most—may change as you go through the process of dying. The child you always thought would be closest to you may now live far away and be less accessible than another child. Or someone you hadn't known too well becomes your most trusted friend in your time of need. Remember, you will need someone to help you at the end. You will need someone to talk to the doctors and make important decisions for you if you become unable to do so yourself.

Support Groups

You can greatly expand your family by finding and joining support groups, if this suits you. Most patients find at least one helpful group, with at least one leader or fellow patient in the group with whom they can make meaningful contact. Support groups are an excellent way to learn more about the technicalities of your disease, what to expect with regard to physical or emotional pitfalls, and methods of coping. Groups may supply more sympathetic and understanding friends than you otherwise would have. There are many patients for whom a support group is a wonderful resource.

Jane R., fifty-two years old, was always an independent soul and didn't socialize much. When she developed breast cancer a few years ago she withdrew even more, because she didn't want to bother her friends with her "problem." But after persistent urging from her daughter, Jane agreed to go to a cancer survivors support-group meeting, where she was initially afraid to even sit down for the start of the meeting. However, after hearing others talk openly of their illness and how they were trying to cope with many different problems, Jane became more relaxed and even talked to some other attendees after the meeting.

In time she became close friends with Susan, a woman about her age who also had breast cancer. Now, four years and many treatments later, she and Susan see each other at least once every week.

As a general rule, it is a mistake to try to hide your illness from the young children in your family. They may not be a part of your "planning committee," but as family members they will be very important participants in what should be a meaningful period of your life. Also, they need to know so that you and they will be able to say good-bye someday in a way that will permit them to remember you with caring and happiness rather than as someone who left them mysteriously. So don't hide from children. They know anyway.

FOR THEIR benefit you owe it to your friends and family to tell them of your diagnosis.

For Family and Friends

IF YOU ARE a member of a patient's family, you need to know as much as possible about the fears, agonies, aspirations, hopes, and goals of your ill loved one. One of the hardest tasks for all of us, physicians included, is to project ourselves into the minds and feelings of patients with a potentially fatal illness. Physicians often think of bodily functions rather than of a patient's feelings or fears, and family and close associates often react in ways that reflect their own fears or concerns about losing a loved one or about death in general. Your task is to focus on the fears, concerns, and desires of your loved one who tells you she has a potentially fatal illness. This is not to say you must abandon all reason and simply support her in whatever way she wishes. But her needs right now are far greater than yours, and what's best for you is what's best for her, the patient.

As difficult as it is for a patient to hear she has a fatal illness, it is often no less difficult for individual members of the family. In fact, sometimes the person with the fatal illness hears and accepts the medical facts with considerably more understanding and rationality than do some members of the family who, in reacting to their own feeling of loss, may be unable to accept the medical facts.

"Never send to know for whom the bell tolls; it tolls for thee." The sum of our existence is the sum of our relationships, and the closer we are to someone, the greater our loss. If we care at all about someone, hearing of his illness invokes in us a dread of loss. If we learn that someone we care for is dying, we feel that a part of us is dying. Our immediate response to the possible loss of a loved one is denial, or a frantic search for methods of preventing the loss. Our reactions are similar to those of the patient, and initially our sense of loss may reflect a concern for ourselves.

Like the patient, if you are to work at planning the best course through the rapids of terminal illness, you need to know the truth. You need to know the diagnosis, the realistic outlook or prognosis, the recommended treatment, and what to expect from it. Your friend doesn't need you to be a physician to her—she has enough of those already. She needs you as a friend and confidant, as someone who not only will listen to her words but will listen beneath her words to what she is saying about her wishes and fears.

You need to deal with your own feelings and fears so that you can look past your potential loss while you are trying to help your relative or friend through her process of dying. However, even while doing this you should not "tell" her; you should listen to her. Of course, if you disagree with any of her important or substantive proposals, such as major treatment or a desire for a form of aid-in-dying, you should and must respond honestly. But present your position in the form of a dialogue or an exchange, as a means of learning, not as a dictum. Above all, don't set limits on your acceptance or love.

If You Disagree with the Plan

If you question your friend's treatment choice, such as surgery instead of chemotherapy, ask her why the doctors are recommending one rather than the other. Remember your limitation of sparse anecdotal experience compared to the total volume of medical knowledge, and avoid undermining your friend's confidence in her treatment. Keep in mind, it is not just the treatment but the match of treatment with a particular and unique patient. What worked for your cousin or a colleague may not work for your friend. See yourself as a resource, as someone who can help dig out useful information.

If you carry preconceived notions of acceptable or "best" end-of-life care, try not to be judgmental with your friend. If your friend tells you she wants to use physician-assisted suicide when things get rough, ask what it is she anticipates being so bad. Maybe you can alleviate her fears and help her avoid the conditions she fears will necessitate aid-in-dying. Help her sift through the multitude of issues.

Avoid invalidating her desires or plans because they don't match what you would do under similar circumstances. If you oppose physician-assisted suicide for religious reasons, get that out, honestly. This is no time for imposing your values, but it is necessary to help her see how her decisions affect you and others. Look for ways to resolve your differences. If you truly want to help her, let her know you will support her in her final decisions. A rift would be the worst outcome for both of you.

> OUR INITIAL reaction to the news of a loved one's fatal illness may be that of self-loss.

Preparing for Caregiving

Begin to prepare for the process and chores of caregiving. Somewhere along the road to death, your loved one will need all the help you can give her. This may become physically, emotionally, and financially difficult for you or others in your family. Think about contingency plans. If she needs more nursing care than the family members can supply, where will she go? If she wants to stay at home to the end, whose home will it be? Keep in mind, a terminal illness narrows the focus of concern and the lives of all who are involved. It can dominate the thoughts and activities of the entire expanded family. If it reaches the extreme, this narrow focus can be unhealthy for everyone. Think about dividing the responsibilities and chores, so that everyone contributes but the process devastates no one. We will discuss this more in Part III.

Summary

1. Tell your friends and family of your diagnosis. You will hurt those you know best if you hide from them when you acquire a fatal illness.

2. Expand your family by finding and joining support groups. They are an excellent way to learn more about the technicalities of your disease, methods of coping, and what to expect with regard to physical or emotional pitfalls.

For Family and Friends

1. Recognize and deal with your sense of potential personal loss, but focus on the fears, concerns, hopes, and goals of your ill loved one. Help her explore her plans and what they will mean to all involved.

2. If you disagree with some part of your loved one's plan, such as opting for assisted suicide, discuss it fully but don't set limits on your acceptance of her.

3. Think about and begin to plan for long-term nursing care at home, in case that becomes necessary. Discuss with other family members potential financial, emotional, and physical burdens and how to deal with them.

PART THREE

Taking Charge When the End Is Near

In this part, we'll discuss how to:

1. Study the probabilities for survival with and without treatments.

2. Keep the dying phase short by stopping curative or life-prolonging therapies by using assisted dying.

3. Obtain optimal comfort care and decide where you want to die: hospital, home, or nursing home.

4. Choose a trusted doctor or nurse to direct your medical care.

5. Be aware of possible end-of-life symptoms and how to deal with them.

6. Address your spiritual and emotional needs.

7. Develop joint decision making with your close family members.

· 10 ·

Understanding the
Last Stages of Life

IN PARTS I and II of this book we explored the need to
plan for eventual dying and then discussed how you might
set your course after getting the bad news of a potentially
terminal illness. We of course hope for a cure, or at least a
prolonged remission with many remaining years of good
life. Ultimately, however, unless we die quickly or unexpectedly, we all will reach the time when seeking a cure
is no longer realistic and we must prepare to direct—or
at least participate in—the medical management of our
dying. In Part III we will discuss the period of weeks or
months of terminal illness that will carry us to the end.

Although this is the time many people dread the most,
if you have done your planning, you have positioned yourself for completing this journey with a minimum of suffering for you and your family, and you will be better
prepared for a peaceful arrival at the end.

In this chapter we will define the terminal phase—how
you know when you are in it and what you can expect
while you're there. We also will discuss using "long-shot"

and alternative treatments as well as planning for terminally ill children.

Defining the Terminal Phase

THE TERMINAL PHASE begins when medical treatment
no longer offers hope for a cure of your disease and by the
best medical assessment you have less than six months to
live. How do doctors know when you've reached this point?
Could they be unaware of potentially curative treatments?
It's possible, but not very likely. There are documented
instances of patients who were told there was no further
curative treatment for them, and who on their own discovered experimental treatments elsewhere—sometimes
out of the country—which gave them further remissions.
However, these are the exceptions that prove the rule.

A new and effective treatment might be discovered
within a few months, but this also is very unlikely. Any
new treatment that is at all promising becomes known
throughout the medical world while it is still in the research phase, long before it is developed to the point of
use with human patients.

Keep in mind that the prognosis of less than six
months to live is a matter of probability and is based on
the general nature of the disease, the particular form of it
you have, how you have responded to treatment, and your
general clinical condition. In practice, doctors do not pro-
nounce a patient "not curable" until all standard curative
treatments have failed and the terminal condition is clini-
cally obvious. With cancer, doctors usually do not give up

on a cure until the expected survival is well under six months, and sometimes under one month.

Every physician has seen patients who are presumed to be in the terminal phase but who then live well beyond six months. Still, the medical determination of less than six months to live is correct most of the time. There is usually no sudden change in a patient's condition to announce the terminal phase. Its arrival comes when curative treatments have failed and the doctors make an educated guess about the time remaining. Also keep in mind that, in practice, most doctors are overly optimistic in the predictions they give to patients.

Facing the Probabilities of the Terminal Phase

WHEN YOU BECOME terminally ill, you should heed well the probability that you will reach the end in less than six months. Given the outlook, you should plan according to your personal hopes, desires, and goals. Since you are dealing with probabilities, not certainties, and since your needs and goals differ from those of the next person, there is no one best plan for you to follow. The first hard decision you must make is whether you want to fight the odds and continue trying for a cure or accept the odds and plan for optimal quality of life during the time remaining. As we have discussed, you don't have to go entirely one way or the other, but the two approaches are so different, and can produce such different outcomes, that your decision now may have a major impact on your process of dying.

When you are in the terminal phase there's not often a good way to hedge your bets and straddle both courses.

To Fight to the End or to Let Go?

What kind of person you are, where you are in your life, how fully and successfully you have lived, how close you are to the natural limits of life, and other life circumstances will all factor into your decisions. In the end, your decisions will reflect how "ready to die" you are. But whatever your condition and whoever you are, you must decide whether to fight your terminal illness or let go of the notion of "beating this disease" and turn your remaining energy to the task of dying as well as possible.

> **MANY PATIENTS disregard the overall odds and "fight" to the end.**

Many older patients, under the weight of terminal illness, are literally too exhausted and weary to want to seek further means of extending their lives. People who see themselves at the end of a long and full life and are truly ready to die may accept the odds and let go of the innately human desire for a cure, so as to go more peacefully to the end.

It is the nature of others, however, perhaps even the majority of patients, to disregard the overall odds and "fight" to the end. If your temperament or goals are best suited to this approach, do it. A forty-year-old mother of young children who has advanced breast cancer and a prognosis of less than six months to live may be willing to take any odds or endure any amount of suffering to extend her life. She may choose experimental therapy with a less than a 10 percent chance of success. A sixty-year-old man with leukemia and a 20 percent chance of a cure with a bone-marrow transplant may be willing to risk these odds in order to live long enough to see the birth of his first grandchild.

But make no mistake, you must understand the odds and what the choices may mean. Patients at the end of life are generally more optimistic about their prospects and the outcomes of therapy than is warranted. If you grasp at every straw, you can push reluctant doctors to futile treatments and procedures they would otherwise not have suggested. When the probability of success of a procedure or treatment is one in ten, be sure to consider what is likely the other nine times.

Using "Long-Shot" and Alternative Treatments

SOME PATIENTS WITH terminal illness adopt a "kill or cure" approach toward medical treatments, which often leads them to take greatly excessive risks. I remember well Elaine, a woman in her late seventies who had cancer of the esophagus and was unable to swallow. Her physicians laid out the options of chemotherapy, radiation therapy, and surgery, and told her she could live about six months more with a feeding tube alone and no other treatment. Despite being told that surgery had only a 5 percent chance of cure with a 25 to 50 percent chance of dying from the operation, she chose surgery. To Elaine, who had worked hard and played hard, life was to be lived fully or not at all. She died in the post-surgery recovery room two days after extensive surgery. I always have thought of this as a case of unnecessarily premature death brought on by the delusion of a cure. Had this woman made a realistic appraisal of her condition and her options, she might have had six more reasonable months before getting to the end. On the other hand, perhaps opting for risky surgery was just Elaine's way of obtaining a quick exit.

APPLY THE SAME reality testing to unconventional treatments that you would to conventional curative therapy.

Going for the cure at all costs often seems reasonable for younger patients who have a potential for longer life if they are cured. But even younger patients need to be realistic, as premature death due to a risky procedure is not a gift to themselves or their family. It's very hard to cross the line between sustaining hope of cure and accepting the reality of dying, but the path to peaceful dying usually requires letting go. And letting go means letting go of the notion of a cure, because doing so is the best way of turning your strength and resources to getting useful living out of your remaining time, with peaceful dying at the end.

Unconventional or Alternative Therapies

At this point in their illness, patients who are unable to accept that there is no cure sometimes look to so-called alternative or unconventional therapies. Since my purpose in writing this book is to help you deal with medical doctors and to attain peaceful dying with the help of mainstream medicine, I am not going to advise you about the multitude of unorthodox therapies and techniques that are available, except to offer a few caveats. First, apply the same reality test to unconventional treatments that you would to conventional curative therapy. Desperately seeking a cure can lead patients to "cures" that, in their false prospect of hope, can be more costly and cruel than any conventional treatment. Endless trips to healers at the four corners of the earth, or attempts to gain control by shifting "responsibility" for the illness and its cure to you and your psyche, can deplete resources and interfere with helpful end-of-life conventional care.

In the end, you must follow your own calling. If you are a person of faith, you may support yourself and your family well with a faith-based form of unconventional healing as an alternative or supplement to conventional medicine. In many cases patients pursue both conventional and unconventional therapies simultaneously. Most physicians are quite willing to have you try diets or supplements, spiritual or psychic engagements, or almost any unconventional "cure" as long as they do not oppose or interfere with conventional treatments. However, if you choose to take an alternative therapy in the form of a chemical or physical substance, tell your regular doctor so that he may advise you of any adverse interaction it may have with your medical therapies.

Many patients find comfort or sustenance in organized therapeutic activities such as laughter, hypnosis, meditation, art or music therapy, visualization of healing forces fighting their diseases, or religious or spiritual activities. These do not conflict with conventional medical treatments and they may be a great aid to you. Just be sure they don't deter you from undergoing the best conventional treatment.

Planning for Terminally Ill Children

WE CANNOT EXPECT a child to think through the ramifications of dying and to make plans for reconciliation and peaceful dying. They are not ready to die and we cannot ask them to assume adult responsibilities for doing so. The legal age for making medical decisions is eighteen, and until then, and probably until a later age for many, the parents or guardian must make decisions and preparations for the child. As a general rule, however, the agonizing trade-offs between curative and palliative therapy hold for children as well as adults. Removal or withdrawal of life-sustaining treatment for children is legally possible, as well as having aggressive palliative care or sedation at the end.

Most children with terminal illnesses receive extensive and sometimes futile treatment at the end of life, and, like adults, many have substantial suffering during the last month of life. The need for aggressive palliative care is as great for children as for adults.[1]

---

1. Joanne Wolfe et al., "Symptoms and Suffering at the End of Life in Children with Cancer," *New England Journal of Medicine*, Feb. 3, 2000, vol. 342, pp. 326–333.

Parents must seek the best medical advice they can get, and counseling for themselves as well as the child. Most pediatric staff and medical centers are well equipped for handling as well as humanly possible the harsh emotional wilderness in which parents of dying children often find themselves.

Summary

1. In the terminal phase, the first hard decision you must make is whether to accept the odds and plan for optimal quality of life in the time remaining or to fight the odds and hope for a cure.

2. In general, patients at the end of life are more optimistic about their prospects and the outcomes of therapy than is warranted.

3. Only you can determine what is the best course of action for yourself, given your clinical condition, your life situation, and your personal beliefs and goals.

4. Apply the same reality testing to unconventional treatments that you would to conventional curative therapy.

5. Supplemental "alternative medicine" may be an aid to you unless it interferes with your getting the best conventional treatment.

6. The agonizing trade-offs between curative and palliative therapy hold for children as well as for adults.

· 11 ·

Strategies for Peaceful Dying

IF YOU HAVE a terminal illness, you may still have many months of good life remaining, but now is the time to plan for a peaceful death. In this chapter we will discuss strategies or methods for attaining peaceful dying. And the key to peaceful dying is peaceful living, with preparation for death.

The Components of Peaceful Dying

TO THE EXTENT you are able to control or direct your dying, what should be your goals for peaceful living during the time you have remaining? Here are some useful guidelines. Some of these goals are yours alone to accomplish, while others you must coordinate with family and your medical providers.

- Instilling good memories
- Uniting with family and medical staff

- Avoiding suffering, with relief of pain and other symptoms
- Maintaining alertness, control, privacy, dignity, and support
- Becoming spiritually ready
- Saying good-bye
- Dying quietly

Thelma: An Example of Peaceful Dying

Although we may think of bad deaths when we think of how people die, most of us also have witnessed some good deaths. I remember Thelma, who was eighty-two years old when she died. Thelma went to see her doctor because of flank pain, and the doctor quickly diagnosed kidney cancer. An operation to remove a large tumor in her left kidney relieved her of her pain, but tests showed that the cancer had spread to her lungs. Also, her one remaining kidney was not working well. Her doctors said she had about six months to live.

Thelma studied the survival statistics her doctors gave her and decided against chemotherapy because the chance of a cure was close to nil. She systematically notified her many family members and friends of her condition and even traveled across the country to visit several dear friends. She and her husband took a cruise to the Caribbean. She became weaker and developed pain when the tumor spread to her bones. She had radiation therapy to her bones, which markedly reduced the pain. With the help of small doses of morphine pills to prevent pain, Thelma remained active.

Many friends and all of her family visited her at home, where she decided she would be at the end, and at every visit she went over old times and shared memories. When she became too weak to take care of herself she enrolled in a hospice plan, and the family hired a professional caregiver to help eight hours a day at home. Toward the end, when she required around-the-clock nursing care, one of her daughters moved into her house to help. Her hospice nurse made frequent visits to determine her needs and to adjust her pain medicines, and her physician kept in touch through the hospice nurse and even went to her home once to visit her.

During family visits Thelma made it quite clear to her children that she would say when she would stop eating and was ready to die. And she made them promise to see that she got enough pain medicine to be comfortable, even if it made her unresponsive or unconscious. She also made sure that the daughter staying with her would have adequate time off to manage her life.

One day Thelma stopped eating, and two days before she died she gathered all her close relatives to her bedside and said good-bye. She asked forgiveness of her children for not being a perfect mother and told them all how much she loved them. She said she was ready to die, and her children told her they would miss her dearly but that it was all right for her to leave.

The hospice nurse began intravenous morphine to counter Thelma's thirst and to keep the pain under control. She slept a lot, but when she awakened she was lucid and pain-free. The next day she exchanged loving good-byes with her husband and soon thereafter closed her eyes and fell asleep. She died four hours later. Thelma had a peaceful death.

Medical Strategies for Peaceful Dying

ANYONE WHO HAS reached the terminal phase has the ability to attain some or all of the components of peaceful dying, given enough time and the necessary planning.

> THE KEY TO peaceful dying is achieving the components of peaceful living during the time you have left.

The three major medical methods for attaining peaceful dying are

1. Keep the dying phase short.
2. Get as much comfort care as it takes to reduce or eliminate symptoms.
3. Select a location that allows for the greatest comfort and peace for dying.

Keeping the Dying Phase Short

The key to minimizing the dying phase is to stop all therapy that prolongs it. As we discussed in chapter 7, when a cure (elimination of the disease) becomes medically unlikely or impossible, the use of "curative" therapy has the potential of drawing out the dying phase. Such prolonging of the dying process, in addition to the discomforting side

effects of the treatments, increases the total time of suffering and decreases the likelihood of peaceful dying.

In order to die peacefully, you must be prepared to let
go of all therapy that might prolong your dying phase. It's
not just "large" treatments such as chemotherapy or surgery that extend the dying process. Often simple and com-
monplace treatments such as antibiotics extend dying and
suffering for weeks or months. Patients in the later stages
of disability from Alzheimer's disease usually have frequent
infections, which, if left untreated, would lead to death.
Families of these patients may be faced with the difficult
decisions of forbearing treatment of infections or of stopping feeding as a means of ending the suffering. It is essential that you give your family instructions and permission
to withhold curative therapy well in advance, if that is
your wish.

If you have reached the terminal phase but need time
for some unfinished business, you may be able to find a
form of treatment that will prolong your life without a
lot of extra suffering. A colleague told me of Virginia, an
eighty-four-year-old woman diagnosed with leukemia,
who was told she had only weeks to live without treatment. Virginia exclaimed, "But I can't die yet—I haven't
finished my memoirs." She and her oncologist settled on a
limited treatment of chemotherapy that gave her some
minor side effects and discomfort for a week, but it sup-
pressed the leukemia for about three months. By then
Virginia had finished her memoirs, and when she again
became sick with the recurring leukemia, she said to her
doctor, "Now I am ready to die." They stopped all medicines, she stopped eating, the visiting nurse made sure she

had enough medicine to suppress all symptoms, and she died in less than a week.

More and more patients, by sharing medical decisions with their doctors, are finding the increasingly successful middle ground of limiting life-prolonging treatments while using aggressive comfort care for a reasonably good quality of life to the end.

Shortening the Dying Phase Through Aid-in-Dying

Depending on your condition and personal values, if your goal is to minimize the dying phase as much as possible you may want to consider aid-in-dying, as discussed in chapter 8. You need not now, or ever, make a decision to use a form of aid-in-dying, but if you want to keep the option open you should begin your preparations now, because later on you may be unable to make decisions. If you are being kept alive with a feeding tube or kidney dialysis, discuss with your doctors and family the possibility of withdrawing this or other forms of life-sustaining therapy when you are in the final phase of dying. Think through your positions on starvation, terminal sedation, and physician-assisted suicide, and decide which are acceptable or unacceptable to you.

Many patients who want physician-assisted suicide as an option wait until life has become intolerable before seeking the necessary pills. By then it may be too late to get help. Keep in mind that it may take many weeks to find a physician willing to work with you or to accumulate the necessary drugs from other sources. Furthermore, under the law in Oregon, there is a mandatory waiting period of fifteen days after the request for physician-assisted suicide before the prescription can be filled. And most physicians who are willing to work with the option of physician-assisted suicide in other states would ask for the same sort of waiting period to prevent someone's making a rash or hasty decision because of a sudden worsening of symptoms that might be relieved by comfort care. The work of peaceful living before dying—saying good-bye to family and friends—also takes weeks and is especially important prior to assisted dying.

PLANNED DEATHS have been successful in achieving the goals of peaceful dying.

Although no state laws mandate a waiting period for withdrawal of life-sustaining treatment such as a feeding tube or artificial ventilator, you can't request withdrawal one day and have it done the next. Physicians need sufficient time first to review your reasoning and present you with other options. They also need to leave enough time for you and your family to say good-bye.

For any form of direct physician-assisted dying you need to plan and be prepared well in advance of the time for doing it. For assisted suicide you must be fully informed in the technique and the potential risks or complications, and you must have the necessary drugs on hand. You must have arrangements for someone to be with you in case of complications. Remember, aggressive comfort care is almost always adequate to control pain and other symptoms during the final phase of dying.

A decision to end your life through assisted suicide should be a morally embedded decision shared with family, and with your physician if possible. Those who choose assisted dying have the opportunity of planning their final good-byes and the advantage of setting the time for them, an advantage often unrealized by patients with unplanned deaths. Most patients who have chosen physician-assisted suicide have been successful in achieving the goals of peaceful dying.

I suggest the following guidelines for any person who pursues any form of aid-in-dying, including assisted suicide:

1. You should be terminally ill with less than six months to live by the best medical estimate.
2. You should be fully informed of your prognosis and fully aware of all options available to you, particularly aggressive comfort care.
3. The method or act must be self-directed, or voluntary.
4. There should be no element of inability to pay for adequate medical care, coercion by others for personal or monetary reasons, or inadequate treatment of a clinical condition such as pain or depression.
5. You should have the understanding and agreement of your closest relatives, with minimal potential for long-term harm or suffering to anyone else from your act.
6. You should not be alone at the end.

Getting Optimal Comfort Care

The second major strategy for optimal dying is to obtain the best possible relief or control of symptoms throughout the dying phase. In medical circles this is known as "aggressive" comfort care. In addition to the use of drugs and other techniques to relieve pain or other symptoms, optimal comfort care means avoiding all procedures that increase pain or discomfort except for an occasional procedure such as putting a tube into a blood vessel for delivering medicines or nourishment.

Unfortunately, evidence shows that many physicians give their dying patients less than optimal relief of pain and other physical symptoms. In some cases doctors neglect altogether this most important part of patient care, often because they do not realize the extent of their patients' suffering.

Many physicians are not trained in or accustomed to giving comfort care. In unspoken medical practice, comfort care is for patients who choose to die at home, in nursing homes, or in hospice programs. Yes, of course, some modern physicians do give wonderful comfort care to patients dying in hospitals, but many of these are generalists, not the specialists who provide most of the high-tech curative care. Even generalists find it hard to buck the "do everything possible" ethic of the hospital, and they often defer to "palliative care specialists" who take over the "comfort care" of patients while curative treatment continues its unyielding course. Many doctors do not see helping their patients die as part of their professional role, and so they avoid any approach to dying patients that does not include repeated attempts to at least prolong life.

The good news, though, is that there has been great improvement recently in the area of comfort care. The vigorous and often heated debate over physician-assisted suicide has heightened the awareness of everyone in the health professions about the need to provide better comfort care for dying patients.

Foundations such as the American Cancer Society and the National Institutes of Health are now directing relatively large grants of money toward research on new techniques of pain control and educating physicians about addressing the comfort needs of their patients. Increasing numbers of physicians are specializing in palliative care or pain control. Hospitals are setting up "comfort care" units. In addition, physicians and lawyers have interpreted the Supreme Court decisions upholding the bans on physician-assisted suicide as endorsing aggressive comfort care even if it unintentionally shortens life.

THE GREAT advantage of optimal comfort care is the quality of life it can give you.

Advanced techniques of pain control and comfort care may result in you dying hours or days earlier than you would otherwise, but this is in fact uncommon. More important, modern techniques can control physical suffering while maintaining reasonable alertness in 90 to 95 percent of patients who are in the last stage of dying. Hospice care, which we will discuss later in this chapter, has improved comfort care immensely for many persons.

Of course, even with optimal comfort care you must not expect a symptom-free ride to the end. Nevertheless, with optimal comfort care you will have much more opportunity to get around and do the things you most want to do in the time remaining. Many patients who have chosen optimal comfort care have said, when close to the end, that the last few months were the happiest they've ever had.

Enough physicians and institutions are willing to provide aggressive comfort care such that, if you plan adequately and assert yourself in asking for it, you can count on this option at the end of life. We will discuss more specific measures of comfort care in chapter 13.

Sudden Changes in Condition

Sudden changes in your condition are more likely when you are in the terminal phase of your illness. If your condition changes slowly, you can implement or alter your plan accordingly. If changes come quickly, you may lose your ability to direct your dying. Some folks remain clear and capable of decision making to the final hour, but for many patients the ability to understand what is happening and to make rational decisions wanes at the end. You can always change your plan, but as of now you should try to set it in place consistent with your goals and projections. Get out your living will and durable power of attorney, reread them, and reconfirm or revise your directives.

Selecting the Best Place for Dying

WHERE DO YOU want to be when you can no longer take care of yourself—at home, in a nursing home or hospice facility, or at the hospital? With any luck you will be able to get around and take care of yourself, perhaps with some assistance from a caregiver, for most of the time after you reach the terminally ill stage. We are now planning ahead for the last few days or weeks or months when a lot or most of the time you will need advanced medical and nursing care. The location you choose for dying may determine how you die, who is with you, and the degree of intimacy and peacefulness of the experience. Choose a location that fits your goals and values and will give you the best chance of achieving them.

The Hospital

If your goal is to minimize the dying phase and maximize peaceful dying with comfort care and time with family, *do not go to the hospital* except for relief of uncontrollable symptoms. Each crisis, and there may be several, will elicit strong appeals from some family members and doctors to go to the hospital to be taken care of. You can do this, but the underlying problem of the advance of your disease won't be fixed; it will simply be deferred. And doing so may make your problems worse.

The mother of a friend of mine was terminally ill with cancer. She was very weak but not in pain and was living at home with the help of her family and a visiting nurse. Over the course of a few days she became unable to swallow anything, and although she said she would prefer to stay at home, after some deliberation the family took her to the hospital. This was a mistake, because instead of her dying in peace at home, the doctors at the hospital operated to insert a feeding tube into her stomach and she lived connected to machines for the last four weeks of her life.

Going to a hospital may mean you won't see your regular doctor, as more and more hospitals are now using "specialists" in hospital care to take care of patients, with help from other specialists. Hospitals are focused on curative treatments, which in turn require often painful and intrusive diagnostic procedures. The need for doctors "to know" what is causing the crisis or a turn for the worse in a dying patient frequently results in their doing procedures that only compound the suffering. The dying patient "has to have" "blood draws" once or twice or three times a day, trips to get X-rays, needles inserted into organs for biopsies, and sometimes operations.

Calling the Medics

Even though the caregivers and family may understand and agree with the patient's plan to die at home, an unanticipated crisis can overwhelm them. Just imagine: The dying patient has been stable for days but suddenly and unexpectedly stops breathing or gasps and falls over. What will happen? What is the reflex we all have? Call the medics! These auxiliary medical personnel are superbly trained to keep patients alive under all conditions, and after arriving and resuscitating someone who has just stopped breathing, what do they do? They take the patient to the hospital. It's their job to do so.

It is very difficult to think in these terms, but if at the end of the dying phase you want to stay out of the hospital, you must instruct your caregivers not to call the

medics if you should suddenly appear to expire, or if you
become unresponsive or unconscious. Yes, each crisis
may indeed be the one that
results in your dying, but you
must be prepared for this if
you choose to die at home.
The time to think all this
through and to make plans is
now, before you have entered
the last phase of dying.

**IF YOUR GOAL is to
maximize peaceful
dying and time with
family, do not go to
the hospital except
for relief of uncon-
trollable symptoms.**

Going to the Hospital for a Specific Reason

There are times, of course, when going to the hospital may
be to your benefit. If you want or need to live a few more
weeks, go for it at whatever the cost. A trip to the hospital
for a procedure or for readjusting medicines may give you
the extra time you need. This is all right. You can know
you are dying and truly let go but still need more time
to say good-bye or to be there for your granddaughter's
wedding.

Another good reason for going to the hospital is to
have a procedure that gives greater symptom relief than
you can get with medicines at home: Blocking a nerve by
injecting or cutting it or decompression of the bowel (a
procedure to prevent bloating and painful distension) may
greatly reduce the amount of painkiller you need at home
without prolonging your dying process. But before you go

to the hospital for a procedure at this stage of your dying, be sure you know exactly what you are going for, and be certain that your caregivers will not allow any additional life-prolonging treatment.

Some of you may prefer to be in a hospital because caregivers are unable to take care of you adequately at home, or because dying at home may place an excessive burden on the family. Some hospitals now have areas where the staff are trained to give comfort care to dying patients, with no life-prolonging treatments. Your regular doctor may be able to take care of you in such a unit.

Otherwise, stay out of hospitals. Once you're in, it's exceedingly difficult to get out. Especially in your weakened and vulnerable condition, you'll be no match for the swarms of bright young doctors ready to do everything possible to prolong your life, and your dying.

Dying at Home

If your goal is peaceful dying among family and friends, the privacy of home is where you want to be. At home you are in familiar territory and with the people you love. Other family, neighbors, and friends can visit you more easily, and you can set the time for meals and the entire agenda for your day, rather than doing it by hospital regulations. Home is where you can have the most control over how you die.

However, being at home also requires caregivers who must look after your medicines, help you to the bathroom, and most likely clean you and take care of your bowel and bladder eliminations toward the end. It may not feel comfortable for you to think of allowing family members to perform chores such as helping you with a bedpan, but they will, often lovingly, and your allowing them to do so can be a gift to them. Most families are able to care for a dying patient at home. It works best when there is twenty-four-hour access to professional services if needed, such as are provided by hospice plans, and periodic "time off" for family caregivers. Both you and your potential caregivers must work through your feelings about it, preferably before the time it becomes necessary.

It is best to have an understanding with your family caregivers that if either you or they feel things are not working well at home, you will hire professional caregivers or move to a medical facility.

> MOST FAMILIES are able to care for a dying loved one at home, especially with professional help, but you must determine in advance whether this is possible and practical.

If hospice or home health agencies are not available to help, the family caregivers alone may not be able to ensure adequate comfort care. The requirements that caregivers possess physical stamina and be able to be absent from jobs and other duties of normal life may make home care impractical or undesirable. In that case, a nursing home convenient to the family may be the best choice.

Getting Hospice Care

Hospice programs offer outstanding comfort care and are covered by Medicare and most insurance plans. The goals of hospice are the same as those we have discussed for peaceful dying: shortening the dying phase by making no further attempts at a cure, providing the best quality of life or comfort care, and dying at home. To enter a hospice program you must be terminally ill with a prognosis of less than six months to live, and you must forgo most curative and hospital care. In this country, there are few hospice in-patient facilities, and hospice care is almost always given in the patient's home. However, many medical centers are setting up areas within hospitals called "palliative care centers" that function much like separate hospice facilities.

If you sign up for a hospice program, your medical insurance (Medicare or other) pays a set per diem fee to the hospice program, which is then responsible for all of your medical care. The philosophy of hospice is to concentrate on the most complete comfort care possible while avoiding any sort of treatment that may prolong the dying phase and thereby make comfort care more difficult. The hospice will not allow curative treatment such as chemotherapy and may even discourage some largely palliative treatments such as blood transfusions. Hospice programs primarily support home care, including advanced methods for pain control. But if you develop pain or another form of suffering that is not controllable at home, most hospices will authorize and finance a limited hospital stay—to get a nerve block, for example—for the purpose of doing whatever is necessary to obtain better comfort care for you.

Talking to Hospice Workers

If you join a hospice program, be prepared to name a primary caregiver—family member, friend, or professional aide—whose responsibility it will be to communicate with and work with the hospice workers. Hospice plans provide access to a multidisciplinary team of physicians, nurses, social workers, clergy, and other health care workers, but you will be treated at home primarily by nurses who will visit you according to your needs. Hospice programs emphasize intense comfort care with family involvement and a focus on the patient's personal and spiritual well-being.

The hospice staff will keep in telephone contact with your regular doctor, who will advise and give medical "orders" for treating you. Hospices have a health professional on call twenty-four hours a day, and all hospices have medical directors who periodically review your case and serve as a backup in case the nurses cannot contact your doctor. Hospice may discourage visits to your doctor as being contrary to the philosophy of handling everything at home.

House calls by physicians are uncommon, although hospice nurses do everything in consultation with your doctor. Practically speaking, with some exceptions, patients who join hospice programs do not see their doctors again. You should be prepared for this shift in professional caregiving. If you intend to choose the hospice option you should discuss this in advance with your primary physician.

Hospice Spiritual and Comfort Care

In most programs, one of the members of the hospice team is a spiritual advisor, usually a member of the clergy. This person will offer to visit you at home for counseling during the last phase of dying, with emphasis on mending relationships. You may accept or refuse this service, depending on your desire.

Most hospice workers will see to it that suffering patients get enough morphine or other drugs to relieve pain or severe discomfort. But even the hospice goal of optimal comfort care does not always ensure peaceful dying. Short of using sedation, not all pain can be relieved in all cases, and other symptoms such as unacceptable side effects of drugs, delirium, or suffocation can sometimes elude the best efforts of hospice workers. Terminal sedation with intravenous barbiturates is done primarily in hospitals, and hospices are unlikely to transfer a dying patient to an in-patient facility. However, some hospice workers and medical directors may be willing to provide this therapy at home.

ALTHOUGH hospice workers see spiritual growth as a very important part of the program, they will not force spirituality on you if you decline.

Dying at home with hospice care has the decided advantage of combining the comfort and privacy of home with the expert provision of comfort care. Many of you will find this the best option. But whether you stay at home or go to a nursing home or hospital when you can no longer take care of yourself is a choice you must make based on your goals, desires, physical needs, and family resources and capabilities.

Going to a Nursing Home

For many terminally ill patients the best place to die is a good nursing home. If your spouse or partner cannot care for you, or if you have been living alone and would need to move to the home of one of your children, the burden of your needs may be too great for the home caregivers. Especially if you can find a good nursing home within easy reach of family and friends, you may find this the best solution.

Look at the following when choosing a nursing home:

- Cost (how much is covered by Medicare or your insurance?)
- Convenience of location for family and friends
- Degree of privacy
- Ability to get hospice-quality comfort care
- Policies on assisted dying, including resuscitation, withholding of therapy, and terminal sedation

It can be difficult to find a nursing home with the right combination of privacy and comfort plus advanced medical care. Nursing homes have their own medical staffs, but many will allow your personal physician to care for you there. As everyone knows, the quality of services varies widely, as does the cost. Finding a good nursing home takes time and effort, so prepare well in advance. Find out about the nursing home's policies on aggressive comfort care and whether they provide it on-site or would send you to a hospital. Within a few years many nursing homes may offer services similar to hospice care. If you want a form of assisted dying, ask about their policies with regard to resuscitation, stopping life-sustaining treatments, or starvation with either morphine or sedation.

Summary

1. Learn what you need to accomplish in order to attain peaceful dying. Some of the essential components of peaceful dying include

- instilling good memories with family and medical staff
- maintaining control at the end
- avoiding suffering
- maintaining alertness
- saying good-bye to your loved ones
- maintaining support for your family
- becoming spiritually ready
- dying quietly with your family beside you

2. Medically prolonged dying may be the greatest obstacle to peaceful dying. The two major methods of avoiding prolonged dying, or keeping the dying phase short, are

- avoiding curative therapies
- using assisted dying if appropriate

3. Achieving optimal comfort care is essential to peaceful dying. Learn the basics of good palliative care and aggressive comfort care.

4. Remember that it is often possible to combine limited curative therapies with optimal comfort care. You do not have to choose totally between one and the other.

5. Based on your personal needs and those of your family, choose the optimal place for dying. Understand the advantages and disadvantages of dying in a hospital, at home, or in a nursing home. With the proper support, the home usually provides the most peaceful setting for dying, while a good nursing home may provide the best setting if home care is not reasonable. Hospitals are geared to curative therapies and prolongation of the dying phase but may be the most secure place for some patients. Consider a hospice inpatient facility or a hospital "palliative care center" if available and appropriate for you.

6. Learn about the comfort care home services of hospice plans. For many, this provides the most peaceful setting for dying.

· 12 ·

Talking to Important
People After You're Ill

As you enter the terminal phase, talking to the important people in your life will be critical to achieving a peaceful death. These people, not necessarily in order of importance, include your doctors, close family and friends, and counselors. In this chapter we will talk about how to share medical decision making with them.

Choosing a Trusted Doctor or Nurse to Direct Your Care

Unless you die unexpectedly and quickly, or are one of the very few persons who receive no medical attention while dying, during the terminal phase you will have innumerable and very meaningful contacts with all sorts of medical professionals. The quality of your interactions with these providers, especially your doctors, will determine to a great degree the quality and duration of your dying process.

In chapter 7 we discussed the advantages of having a

trusted physician be your spokesperson for your major medical decisions. The idea was to choose one physician who would not be driven solely by what was medically possible but who knew you well enough to supervise your care according to your overall needs and desires.

By now in the course of your illness you may have a different set of doctors from the group you had a year or just six months ago. Unless you have foregone curative therapy from the start of your illness, you have met one or many specialists who have directed much of your care. If you have cancer, you may see an oncologist more than you see your primary doctor. Or, if you have had a stroke, you may relate most to a neurologist or to a rehabilitation doctor. Frequently you have not chosen these experts who have been "called in on the case" by your primary doctor or another expert. If you have had hospital stays, you may have met a bewildering number of nutritionists, medical residents and interns, nurse practitioners, physicians' assistants, physical therapists, respiratory therapists, and many others.

You will probably form a close relationship with a provider who will naturally assume the role of your trusted advisor, but sometimes the division of medical care among specialists leaves a terminally ill patient with no one who will act as coordinator of all care. If you have a trusted primary-care physician whom you want as your ultimate medical advisor, ask him to stick with you to the end. Not many will refuse such a personal request.

Or you might choose someone other than a physician to take a leading role in working with you in planning your care from now to the end. Many patients, with or without hospice involvement, find themselves most comfortable working closely with caring, compassionate, and effective nurses or social workers. If you are lucky enough to have a family member in the health professions, you might want that person to coordinate your medical care. It's also a good idea to keep the person you've chosen to be your attorney-in-fact for health care fully informed of your desires, directives, medical condition, and treatments.

Talking with Your Doctors

REGARDLESS OF WHOM you choose to coordinate your medical care, continue talking to your doctors—all of them. If you make your wishes known to all of them, there's less chance of any one of them acting contrary to your desires. Ultimately, you want to have some control over how and when you die—enough to be able to stop needless suffering at the end. The best means of attaining this goal is sharing control with your doctors, each seeking the wisdom of the other in making decisions. But after a long series of shared decisions in the management of your dying, in the end the last decision should be yours.

Many physicians will have anticipated your need to discuss end-of-life issues, and your doctor may initiate the subject before you do. If so, all the better, but be prepared to do it yourself. At your next visit take a checklist of the subjects or questions you need to cover, and have someone with you to help ask questions. If necessary, tape-record the discussion with your doctor, explaining to her that you have trouble remembering and understanding what she tells you. Recording a discussion may make your doctor more cautious, so be prepared to ask a lot of specific questions and add statements such as "I just want to be able to refer to what you have said, doctor, and I will take your comments as advice, not as absolute facts."

Reviewing Your Goals

If you wish to have all possible curative treatments regardless of their likelihood of success, be sure your doctors understand this in advance. However, if your goal is peaceful dying, first and foremost let your doctors know that you understand your condition and wish to avoid any treatment designed to prolong your life. You might say to your doctor, "I know I am dying, and I appreciate all you have done to help me. But now my goal is to die peacefully. It's all right for you not to use treatments to prolong my life any more." Another approach is to write or type a statement for your doctor in which you state your wish to avoid life-prolonging treatments, and then write, "I give you permission not to prolong my life." Believe me, a simple statement like that will give you the necessary understanding with most doctors. If you've done your planning, your doctor won't object.

THE BEST MEANS of attaining your goal of a peaceful death is sharing control with your doctors, each seeking the wisdom of the other in making decisions.

Next, get out a copy of your living will and durable

power of attorney and discuss the major points with your doctor. If more than one doctor is making major decisions, go over these documents with all of them and be sure copies are in the records of all the institutions you may enter—clinics, hospitals, nursing homes, hospice. If any doctor hesitates or disagrees with any stipulation, give your reasons for and feelings about what you are requesting. Tell your doctors you expect their compliance with your end-of-life requests for medical treatment. If you cannot reach agreement with one or more doctors now, you may need to work around them or even get a new doctor. Your advance directives are the bedrock foundation for how you want to die. Also, give your family and doctors a worksheet with your goals and preferences for treatment if you suffer brain damage, coma, or cardiac arrest.

Palliative Care

Talk about palliative care. Let your doctor know your preference if the required amount of drugs results in a necessary choice between complete relief of pain and alertness. For example, you could ask your doctor, "If I am having a lot of pain, will you be willing to give me enough painkillers to make me comfortable, even if it takes so much it knocks me out?" Your doctor may answer, "Yes, of course," but you have to ask the question to get the doctor's commitment. By asking if she will give you enough to keep you comfortable you are signaling a desire for her to let you determine when and how much pain medicine is enough, on an ongoing basis. Otherwise she might assume you want the least amount of painkiller possible, so as to avoid drowsiness or development of tolerance to the drug. And don't worry about broaching the subject in advance—both you and your doctor have a better chance of doing it right when the time comes if you have had prior discussions.

When you first learned your diagnosis and had some time to think about it, you may have talked to your doctor about many things, including your fears. Bring up your fears again. Even the patient at peace with dying has fears. One person is afraid of uncontrolled pain, while another is afraid of losing insurance coverage for home care or hospice. Yet another person fears losing mental capacity and thereby the ability to direct matters at the end. The fears you have now may be quite different from the ones you had after learning your diagnosis. No one else knows them unless you share them. Your doctors may be able to reassure you about some or all of them, and they will be more prepared to deal with the conditions or complications you've identified.

Talking to Your Doctor About Aid-in-Dying

If you want the option of starvation, terminal sedation, or physician-assisted suicide at the end, say so in clear language. If you just hint at what you want, you probably won't get it. If you say something like: "Doctor, if things get really tough for me and you can't control the pain, do you think you could give me something stronger?" the doctor may not understand what you are asking. Tell her how far you want to go toward unconsciousness if you are suffering. Ask your doctor if she will be ready and willing to give you enough painkillers or sedatives to eliminate hunger or thirst after stopping food and water. Ask her if she will be willing to sedate you to unconsciousness during fasting if you should so choose. Ask her if she will honor the same request of your attorney-in-fact, or your family, if you become incapable of making decisions.

> **ASK YOUR DOCTOR**
>
> "If I am having a lot of pain, will you be willing to give me enough painkillers to make me comfortable, even if it knocks me out?"

If you want physician-assisted suicide, ask if and how you can get the necessary drugs. Tell your doctor you must prepare now, not later, even though you may never use the drugs. Ask how to take the drugs, and if she doesn't know how, ask her to find out. Talk about your plans and desires. If you don't get the answers you want, say so. If you have serious disagreement with your doctor over a major element of your end-of-life plan, consider changing doctors.

Talking with Your Family

NOW ESPECIALLY YOU need your family to help you plan wisely and effectively. You and your family will want to act interdependently in planning and implementing end-of-life care—and in caring for each other.

You must let your family know of your readiness to die. They may not understand your condition or share your decision to let go. They do not want to lose you, and some of them may do anything possible to avoid facing this reality. If you are to resist their incessant and persuasive pleas for further attempts at a cure, you must share with them your reasons and determination to let go, if this is your decision. Your family may oppose you and try to change your mind, but this is their duty as they see it. The best way they know of helping you in your battle against dying is to give you assurances that they will do anything and everything possible to keep you alive. What haunts family perhaps more than anything after a loved one has died is the feeling of guilt over having done "too little" when there was a chance to help. Tell them that they and your doctors already have done everything remotely possible to reverse your course and now it is time to work on another level.

Bringing Your Family into Your Orbit

Your family needs your permission to become involved in your planning. Although some family members always may have tried to tell you what to do, most need you to tell them directly that you want their wisdom and help in making important decisions that will influence how and where you die. If your family members are not involved in decision making and discussions about the end of life now, they will not feel involved at the end. Do not even think of sparing them the grief and distress of your condition—to do so would deprive them and you of being united and peaceful at the end.

Tell your family and close friends about your disease and condition so they can better understand your reasoning. Tell them your hope is to consummate your life with their companionship and blessing, although you are willing to listen to their concerns. Forthright talking gives you and your family the best means of exploring everyone's desires, fears, reasons, and expectations. Your talks may be difficult or even agonizing, but if they are open and honest they will give you the closeness with your family that you need for peaceful dying.

Go over with your family everything you have discussed or will discuss with your doctors. Tell the family your decision, or thoughts, about dying in a nursing home, in the hospital, or at home, and how you feel about hospice. Plan with them whom they should notify about your condition, and how much to tell friends and neighbors outside your inner circle. Remind them of your living will and durable power of attorney. Discuss your concerns about pain or other physical symptoms, and tell them how aggressively you want to use painkillers, if necessary.

Tell your loved ones everything you want them to remember after you leave them. Bring them into your room, one by one or in groups, and recall with them the shared experiences you most value, which will best help them to remember you in a positive way. Ask them to forgive your past imperfections or wrongs in dealing with them, and tell them you forgive theirs. Connecting with your family at this time is the best way of showing your love for them, and of giving the emotional peace you need now and your family will need after you leave.

If it seems right, make a video of your most cherished remembrances of them, so that they will always be able to see and hear you. While you're at it, draw up a list of instructions for business you want them to execute after you leave, including funeral arrangements. You might even arrange to have flowers sent to your caretakers, with a note from you, on the anniversary of your departure.

The Impact of Your Illness on Your Family

How has your illness changed your family's lives? How will it? Most family members can arrange to give help for a brief illness, but not many are able to set aside their usual lives for months. Will one person, commonly a daughter, bear a disproportionate burden of the necessary caregiving? Will her children, your grandchildren, lose necessary attention and care? Will your plans mean loss of a job or a special experience or perhaps a courtship for one of your home caregivers? Is anyone already burning out because she must stay by your bedside twenty-four hours a day, seven days a week? Will your family caregivers need additional help, especially for physical tasks such as bathing or cleaning you? Are there

NOW YOU NEED your family more than ever to help carry out your plans. Bring them into your orbit.

major unreimbursable expenses of your home health care that would be covered by insurance if you were in a hospice or nursing home? Will your loved ones have the emotional and physical stamina to be with you for a week or more of starvation or terminal sedation?

Alternatively, if you choose not to stay at home will you be giving your family insufficient opportunity to express their love by caring for you? Remember, most families are able to care for a dying loved one at home, if they have sufficient help. And, for many family members, caregiving is a gift they want to give.

We tend to keep most in mind the memories last acquired, and a family member's sharp images of the last few weeks of a loved one's physical and spiritual disintegration may forever overlay the mental recordings of a lifetime of shared accomplishment. If you worry about your family's last memories of you, tell them your concerns. Let them know it is all right for them to allow professional caregivers to do the more distressing jobs so their memories will not be overwhelmed with despair.

Talking to Your Family About Aggressive Comfort Care

If you want the option of aggressive comfort care to the point of intermittent loss of consciousness, or starvation with or without terminal sedation, discuss it in advance with your family. One or more of them may have to make arrangements if one of these treatments becomes necessary, and if they do not know your wishes in advance they may not implement them soon enough, if at all. All medical procedures take time to get started, and your caregivers must be able to anticipate your needs.

Your loved ones know you are dying but are not ready to lose you. They often push for what are in fact futile treatments because they don't know how to "let go" and allow you to die. Be sure they understand that your plans are conditional. For example, if pain and discomfort become intolerable, you will want them to help you with aggressive pain medication. If you get to the point of wanting to bring things to a close, you will want them to help you in fasting or terminal sedation. These techniques are personally challenging and they denote a finality that most family members are unprepared for. You must give them time to deal emotionally not just with losing you but with a particular form of dying, before you implement it. If you think you cannot adequately discuss these matters individually with one or more family members, you can arrange to have a group meeting at which you present your plans to all your loved ones at once. Family members who understand and support you can assist you in presenting your plans to other family members. You might even arrange to have a counselor assist you at a group meeting.

Talking to Your Family About Aid-in-Dying

It is absolutely imperative that you talk to your family about your wishes regarding resuscitation, withdrawal of life-sustaining therapy, or physician-assisted suicide. Loved ones not included in your decision about assisted dying may feel that they were excluded from your trust at the end. They may carry with them forever the feeling that you abandoned them if you used a form of assisted dying without their knowing it and they didn't have their chance to say good-bye. A family member who did not know of the patient's plan to be disconnected from a ventilator may forever feel that with a little more family support the patient might not have felt compelled to die that way.

Find out how family members feel about your plans for assisted dying and allow them to give full expression to their concerns and fears. Ask how they will feel a year later, or ten years later, if you implement the option of physician-assisted suicide. If you think they will resist this plan, that is all the more reason to talk to them. Talking with them will help you check your reasons for wanting to do it. Their resistance might be an expression of their fear of losing you, but they may support you once they have had enough time to work through their feelings and realize they are going to lose you anyway.

Whatever you do, don't use any means to end your life without talking with your family. The key to spiritually and emotionally peaceful dying is connecting with your family before the end. The person who puts a bullet through his head "to save everyone the grief of my slow and painful dying" is committing the ultimate disconnect. It may solve a problem for the dying patient, but it leaves the family with insoluble and enduring emotional pain.

By including family members in your discussions you have allowed them to express their love, evident even when they are opposing your plans. Although they may regret your act, they may be able to live with your decision because it is yours and they love you. You have relieved them of the burden of being responsible for the moral decision.

A good death takes time—give yourself and your loved ones enough time to reconcile differences.

Summary

1. Talk to the people in your life—your doctors, close family and friends, and counselors—who will share medical decision making with you.

2. Choose a trusted doctor or other health care provider to be your medical spokesperson in keeping your medical care consistent with your goals.

3. Tell your doctor that at some point you may wish to stop life-sustaining treatments. Let her know where you want to die.

4. If you want to have assisted dying as an option at the end, tell your doctor in clear and unambiguous language and make arrangements for getting the necessary medical assistance.

5. Make it clear to your doctors and other providers that at the end the last decision should be yours.

6. Let your family know of your readiness to die, so they can achieve their own emotional acceptance of your desires and needs.

7. Bring your loved ones into your orbit and allow them to become involved in your planning.

8. Talk to your loved ones about the burdens of caregiving.

9. Discuss with all close family members or friends how you want to manage end-of-life comfort care as well as the possibility of a form of assisted dying.

· 13 ·

Dealing with
Symptoms During
the Terminal Phase

Unless you die suddenly, as in an accident or from unexpected cardiac arrest or stroke, your disease will produce symptoms and disabilities. The type, severity, and characteristics of your symptoms are the result of your particular disease and of your response to treatment. In turn, your symptoms and how they affect you will in large measure determine how distressfully or peacefully you die.

Two patients with the same disease can have quite different symptoms. For example, although Lisa has leukemia, she suffers only from mild weakness due to anemia. She has two courses of chemotherapy with moderate symptoms but improves a lot after each course and lives a fairly normal life. About a year after learning of her diagnosis, she dies suddenly at home of a stroke. Paul has the same disease, but in addition to having more severe fatigue, he has one infection after another, with fever, chills, and many hospitalizations. He also has two courses of chemotherapy, both of which cause extreme symptoms and disability.

He slowly declines and, about a year after learning of his diagnosis, he dies after spending two weeks in the hospital.

Lisa and Paul had vastly different reactions to the same disease, and their different symptoms determined their quality of living and dying. How you deal with your symptoms will be a large factor in how peacefully you live till the end.

Dealing with Physical Distress

PAIN IS THE physical symptom most of us associate with slow dying, but other physical symptoms can be equally distressing and sometimes harder to relieve—weakness being the most frequent.

Weakness

Modern medicine does not have a good treatment for extreme weakness. Some dying patients are so severely fatigued that they can hardly raise a finger. There is no antidote for being unable to get in and out of the bathtub, or being too weak even to get in and out of bed. The only medicine for this is the help of others. If you develop extreme fatigue, do not berate yourself for "doing nothing to get stronger." Sometimes a blood transfusion can bring relief from extreme fatigue or weakness, and some drugs can increase alertness, but for many patients there are no drugs or stimulants that reliably enable them to overcome the extreme debility of disease or its frequent bedfellows—confusion and anxiety.

Breathlessness

Severe and persistent shortness of breath is very common in patients whose disease involves the lungs (and windpipe) or the heart. The medical term for shortness of breath is dyspnea, literally "difficulty in breathing." In some cases there is a specific physical problem that can be corrected. For example, collection of fluid around the lungs or the heart can compress these organs, causing shortness of breath, and removal of the fluid through a needle can relieve the problem. Similarly, radiation therapy to shrink a tumor pushing on the heart or lungs can be very effective in relieving shortness of breath. Sometimes a drug such as cortisone can alleviate a severe lung problem.

Morphine often can alleviate severe shortness of breath despite its potential for suppressing the natural breathing drive. The risk that morphine or similar drugs will stop breathing altogether is overstated and unnecessarily feared when the drug is administered in doses necessary to suppress symptoms. In fact, physicians probably underuse morphine as treatment for severe shortness of breath.

Other Physical Symptoms

Other demeaning and debilitating physical conditions that often occur during the dying phase include nausea and vomiting, fever, putrid-smelling wound infections, diarrhea, and loss of bowel and bladder function. Granted, these wretched problems can lead to despair, but modern palliative care experts can minimize them through a variety of treatments; you need not endure such physical suffering. If at the end the

THE BOTTOM LINE is, if you have pain and need relief, ask for it, loud and clear.

problem is extreme and available methods prove to be insufficient, enough morphine or sedation can relieve you of any physical symptoms by inducing a coma or near-coma. Keep in mind, pain is not the only physical problem from which you may obtain relief through sufficient drugs.

Getting Good Pain Relief

THERE SHOULD BE no barrier to adequate pain relief. Unfortunately, many patients still receive inadequate comfort care and pain relief. Too many physicians remain poorly trained in pain control and harbor excessive fears that they will cause addiction of their patients by prescribing narcotics for pain relief. In addition, physicians fear disciplinary reprisal from professional or government authorities for dispensing narcotics.

But the climate has changed. Articles on the need for better pain control are now in almost every medical journal they pick up, and pain control is one of the leading subjects in continuing education courses for physicians. Physicians are learning that adequate pain control almost never results in addiction. In addition, the legal atmosphere has changed. From the Supreme Court down, there is recognition of the legality of aggressive comfort care for end-of-life patients, even to the extent of shortening the last stage of dying as an unintended consequence of treatment.

In fact, negligence lawsuits have been brought against physicians for not adequately responding to patients' needs for pain relief. Some advocates of aggressive palliative care have even suggested disciplinary action against physicians who do not give adequate pain relief.

The bottom line is, if you have pain and need relief, ask for it, loud and clear. I am not trying to shift all responsibility to you, the already suffering patient, but I am telling you to at least make known your need. If you're already getting pain medicine but it isn't enough to make you comfortable, say so in unambiguous terms. If you say, "Well, maybe I'm having a little pain" when you really are having a lot of pain, "well maybe" you'll get some extra painkiller, and "maybe" you won't. Doctors are only human, and they can't guess how much you are hurting. And they haven't lived with you for thirty years, and so they don't know how to interpret your "nice" ways of asking for something without wanting to bother anyone. You must be direct and explicit.

Getting Pain Relief Early

Pain can persist for weeks or months; don't put off treating it until it gets "worse" or becomes "too much to take." In fact, it's best to treat pain effectively from the start, when it's easier to control. It will then be easier to "stay on top of it" if it becomes more severe. Experts in comfort care aim for continuous treatment in order to avoid episodes of severe pain, rather than waiting for a bad spell before treating. The more effective your pain control is in the beginning, the better your chance of living longer, comfortably. Don't hesitate to ask for relief of pain that is "bearable" but uncomfortable.

If you have continuous pain, you need continuous, seamless relief. Pain medication for routine use is available in the form of pills to swallow, suppositories to insert into the rectum, patches to apply to the skin, liquids to spray into your mouth, or injections. These preparations are effective for continuous relief if given before pain recurs and before the prior dose has worn off. Some of the skin patches are particularly effective in giving around-the-clock relief. But physicians don't know what dose of drug is sufficient for you and how often you require it. Your needs can change either way, so you must keep your physicians regularly informed. Be aware that some physicians suspect that many patients ask for greater amounts of painkillers than are necessary to relieve their pain. Describe your pain as accurately as you can. If you are known for not crying wolf, your request will be all the more noticeable.

Patient-Controlled Analgesia

One technique for customizing pain relief is called *patient-controlled analgesia,* or PCA. A plastic tube is inserted under the patient's skin or into a vein to allow an infusion of a painkilling drug continuously or at intervals. At any time you, the patient, can manually press a button to administer an additional dose of the painkiller. If and when you feel a return of pain, you can immediately push the button to receive the next dose in time to reverse the build-up of pain. If, on the other hand, you feel too drugged or sedated, you can reduce the flow of the drug to the dosage you need or desire. You can have as much as you need to control your pain.

IT IS BETTER to treat pain from the beginning instead of waiting until it gets worse.

Unfortunately, PCA can be expensive and you need to determine whether your insurance or personal resources will support the expense.

The Limits to Optimal Comfort Care

Because physical activity usually increases pain, you may not be able to regain your normal activity level. However, with good pain control your overall energy level should improve and the decrease in debilitating fatigue should allow you to undertake and enjoy sedentary activities like talking with friends or riding in an automobile.

A second limitation of aggressive comfort care is that you might be tempted to use it to palliate the angst of dying. If you use drugs to alleviate your emotional despair and your grief about dying, you may lose the opportunity to do important spiritual and interpersonal work. The trick—far from an easy one—is to judge when you are getting close to the point when the amount of pain medication you require infringes on your emotional and mental capacity. This is when you lose your ability to make decisions and to say good-bye.

The Minimal Risk of Addiction or Overdose

For many patients, good, continuous, and ongoing control of pain actually reduces the amount of drugs they require overall; it does not lead to their taking ever-increasing amounts. Some reduction in effectiveness (tolerance or habituation) does occur, but there's nothing wrong with taking higher doses when necessary, and doing so will not by itself lead to reduced effectiveness of the drugs.

Addiction is not a legitimate issue here. Addiction means antisocial and illegal behavior when there is no medical need for the drug. A true patient can become habituated but not addicted. If the cause of pain is removed, a true patient can get off narcotic drugs in about a month, without addiction. As a patient you need drugs for a specific medical purpose—pain relief—and the drugs will help improve your physical function, not worsen it. You may require drugs for relief to the end, but you will not become a junkie. The notion of addiction is immaterial—the purpose is comfort care, not support of a drug habit.

Death by accidental drug overdose is a very rare occurrence among patients being treated for comfort care. People who overdose on street drugs are often getting unpurified drugs and are taking them in relatively high doses that produce sudden changes. Even among those 5 to 10 percent of dying cancer patients who cannot get adequate relief without being drugged to unconsciousness, the increases in dosage are gradual and not sudden enough to abruptly end life.

If you get to the point of unmanageable pain, it is entirely within your rights, as well as medically and legally acceptable, to ask for drug-induced unconsciousness, or terminal sedation. However, if you reach this point, please understand that your alertness and decision-making capacity already will be greatly impaired or absent, and so you must have prepared in advance for your caregivers to carry out your wishes.

Other Methods of Pain Control

PHYSICIANS SOMETIMES USE other methods of pain control instead of or as a supplement to narcotic drugs. Stimulation of the skin with a soft cloth or a battery-powered electrical stimulator can be successful in treating pain from phantom limbs (after amputation) or for pain in the arms or legs. Injecting an anesthetic drug into the area of a nerve can "block" pain impulses in the same way dentists provide pain relief by blocking nerves to your teeth. Stimulating a nerve with a continuous and painless electrical current can also block the pain sensation traveling through that nerve. In extreme cases, surgery can be used to destroy nerves, either by cutting or electrical destruction of tissue. This technique often provides good relief, although long-lasting benefit is less common. Finally, medical researchers are developing new methods using antibodies or chemicals to destroy nerves whose function is to transmit pain. If conventional drug therapy does not give adequate comfort, ask your doctor if one of these procedures might help.

Most major medical centers now have pain clinics

or services, staffed by physicians whose specialty is comfort care. If you are not getting adequate pain control ask your doctor to refer you to a pain management clinic or to a pain specialist.

OTHER procedures, such as nerve blocks or skin stimulation, can be successful in some cases when conventional drug therapy does not give adequate comfort.

Pain may have a major psychological component, and some patients get considerable relief from unconventional treatments such as relaxation techniques, laughter, music, skin stimulation or touch therapy, or acupuncture. Antidepressant medications may be very effective in reducing pain or other types of discomfort. Any techniques that help are worth pursuing simultaneously with conventional medical comfort care.

Dealing with Mental or Emotional Distress

JUST AS YOU will need physical comfort during your terminal illness, so you will also need emotional and spiritual comfort. Emotional comfort care may be every bit as important as physical comfort care.

Although some dying persons may welcome death as a release from intense physical or emotional suffering, and some may peacefully accept death as God's will, it is hard to conceive of a circumstance in which death is not accompanied by mental anguish. It is, after all, the end of all we cherish, all that we are.

Depression Can Be a Natural Reaction

Symptoms of clinical depression—such as sadness, crying, and lack of interest in family and friends—are common in people with a terminal illness and are a normal reaction to dying. It is also common to have physical symptoms such as weight loss, fatigue, and loss of interest in sex. Although these symptoms are due to the underlying disease they are the same as symptoms experienced by people who are not dying but have the emotional problem of depression. Because of this similarity in symptoms, it is difficult if not impossible for physicians to know whether depression in a dying patient is a natural grieving for the loss of one's life or is actually due to an unrelated but treatable emotional disorder.

If depression is a natural reaction to dying, treatment with antidepressants may be unsuccessful and can possibly cause unwanted side effects. But I remember one patient, Mary K., who was extremely depressed when she became terminally ill. She had had a history of depression some ten years before, and when she was treated with antidepressants her mental outlook improved substantially and she was much better able to cope with the process of dying.

How an individual reacts emotionally to the process of dying is a function of his attitudes, values, and choices. For example, one patient with lung cancer may go through the entire dying process without any outward signs of depression while another patient with the same disease and equivalent physical symptoms and disability may be depressed to the point of suicide. Although it is possible that the depressed patient has acquired a second clinical disorder—depression—in addition to cancer, it is also possible that the difference in the way the two patients react emotionally to their cancer is because of their personalities and beliefs. Strong spiritual or religious beliefs may be a buffer against feelings of depression, whereas dying patients without strong spiritual beliefs may feel and deal with their sadness by expressing it more openly.

Getting Help with Depression

Regardless of whether one can have control over one's reaction to disease and dying, whether the reaction or illness is driven mostly by physical and chemical changes, or whether one's emotional reaction to a fatal disease is a reflection of one's personality, certain methods and techniques of coping may be very helpful to you.

Many dying patients work out their grief during the course of their dying process by accepting the fate of dying, by reconciling with friends and family, and by coming to terms with their spiritual beliefs. Spiritual growth—finding meaning in your life and death—is a component of peaceful dying. Many patients gain spiritual or emotional comfort by talking with a trusted friend or member of the clergy. Some benefit greatly from talking to a professional counselor. Psychotherapy may be a very useful form of emotional comfort care for coping with personal problems at the end of life. If you feel more depressed than seems appropriate, talk to your doctor; there may be a way to help you with this emotional problem.

As you proceed through the terminally ill phase, be aware of the immense help you can gain from talking to family or professionals about the harsh emotional realities you will face.

Summary

1. Treat pain from the beginning instead of waiting until it gets "worse" or becomes "too much to take." Keep your physicians regularly informed of your needs for relief of pain or other symptoms.

2. Drugs for comfort care help you function physically better, not worse—addiction is not an issue.

3. Consider the use of "patient-controlled analgesia," or PCA.

4. Understand that even with optimal comfort care you may not be able to regain your normal activity level.

5. Consider procedures such as nerve blocks or skin stimulation if conventional drug therapy does not give adequate comfort.

6. Use unconventional treatments such as relaxation techniques, laughter, music, touch therapy, or acupuncture, if one of these suits you.

7. If you are not getting adequate pain control, ask your doctor to refer you to a pain management clinic or pain specialist.

8. A depressed mood and symptoms of clinical depression are common in people with a terminal illness and are a normal reaction to dying.

9. If you feel more depressed than seems appropriate, consider talking with a trusted friend, member of the clergy, or professional counselor.

· 14 ·

Arriving at the End

As you approach the end, you may suddenly or gradually lose the ability to make decisions. You must therefore have a prior understanding with your caregivers of the point at which you would wish implementation of aggressive comfort care, terminal sedation, or any form of assisted dying. Dying is a medically managed process with or without your control of it, but your plan will be most honored and your comfort at the end will be best if your family are in constant touch with your professional caregivers. What is best for you is your way.

Symptoms at the End

For those who don't lapse into a coma or die without warning, there can be periods of increased symptoms at the end. It is common to feel severely fatigued and confused during the week before death. Many dying persons hallucinate about being a child or talking to loved ones long dead. Other common symptoms at the end include generalized weakness, confusion, restlessness, anxiety, an increase in pain, seeing less well, being short of breath with irregular breathing (or air-hunger), and having trouble clearing saliva from the throat. Sometimes people lose control of their bladder or bowels. During the last day of life most patients feel too weak to get out of bed and are unable to eat; many have difficulty recognizing family members.

Patients who are dying slowly often lose their appetite days or weeks before the end. This is a natural reaction to the dying process, but family members and friends may not understand this. They may think your not eating means you are giving up. In fact, you may have a conflict with your loved ones over how much you should eat. This "battle of eating" is symbolic to the onlookers who may still think they can nourish you back to better health. This is not worth fighting about. It's OK not to eat. Explain to your family and friends that this is nature's way of closure, that eating more than feels right to you will make you more uncomfortable.

Unusual Phenomena

Some dying persons experience extraordinary phenomena during the last few moments of life. Some "see" their siblings or parents who died long ago. Some hear "music from heaven" or see images of the afterlife or a large, bright light beckoning them upward. Whether these experiences are previews of the afterlife or biochemical phenomena in a blood-deprived brain, they seem to be pleasant and personally fulfilling and may give meaning to the departing patient. They also may comfort the members of the dying person's family, who see their loved one depart in relative peace.

Many dying persons are aware of very little of what is happening around them. They respond only to the strongest stimulus—pain. If pain control is adequate, this terminal phase of half-consciousness can be a period of serenity, although for some patients this "serene" phase lasts for a matter of minutes following many days of physical and emotional disintegration. Although lucidity and serenity may accompany you to the end, you would be wise not to count on it without planning for aggressive comfort care if necessary.

Dealing with Intractable or Prolonged Suffering

IF THE END is at hand and your physical symptoms are becoming uncontrollable, you may say your good-byes and request enough medicine to abolish all suffering. You and your family must be forceful and insistent in getting sufficient medicine to achieve continuous and uninterrupted symptom relief.

Some patients with inadequate comfort care go through cycles of pain (or other symptoms such as shortness of breath) alternating with coma induced by drugs. With each cycle of pain the patient is given enough additional narcotic medicine by mouth, skin patch, or injection to fall asleep, but after a few hours she awakens crying out from the return of pain. Another, larger dose of the drug is ordered and given, just enough to induce calm and sleep for a few hours, until the cycle repeats.

This cycle is avoidable. You must have family and medical providers agree in advance that you will get enough medicine to eliminate all suffering at the end. This means no swings in and out of consciousness and sensation of suffering. It means an uninterrupted and peaceful sleep to the end.

IF YOU ARE within a day or two of the end you do not need assisted dying—aggressive comfort care with or without sedation can give you a peaceful death.

Medical caregivers often favor narcotics given through skin patches or by rectal suppositories because they are easier to apply and the dosage is more controllable, but it is sometimes difficult to increase, or "turn up," the dosage enough by these means. Be prepared to ask for an intravenous infusion of the drug to give sufficient control.

Avoiding All Pain

If you want to avoid all pain at the end, insist that if sensation and suffering begin to return a family caregiver or nurse can immediately increase the dosage until it is adequate to eliminate all sensation. Not only is this doable, you have the right to it. You can remain in a drug-induced coma (no sensation) for days, if necessary. It is like sleep. Narcotics are not always able to induce continuous coma, so plan in advance for your medical caregivers to use a sedative to induce sleep if necessary.

Even in hospice programs, an unfortunate few patients may linger weeks while passing in and out of semi-consciousness with enough medicine to eliminate most of the pain most of the time. The unfortunate patient and family are achieving neither a peaceful last phase of life nor a merciful death. If you are facing days or weeks of severe symptoms that aren't controllable by narcotics, or cycles of coma alternating with symptoms, ask for terminal sedation. Fortunately, many physicians are willing to use this approach if the patient and family are unanimous in their request for it.

If you have a day or two at most to live, there is no need for one of the methods of assisted dying, such as withdrawing a feeding tube or assisted suicide. At this point, so close to the end, aggressive comfort care with or without continuous unconsciousness can give you a peaceful death.

If You Are a Friend or Family Member: Caring at the End

AT THE END all family members become consummate caregivers. If one person has been the major caregiver, others should be careful not to usurp that person's role at the end. If you rush in at the last moment and try to take control, you could upset the finely tuned dynamic of communication that the primary caregiver and patient have established during the last few days.

Providing Good Comfort Care

Your prime effort as a family member or friend should be to assist your loved one in meeting her goals. First on the list is provision of good comfort care. Pain or fear of a terrible death will undermine all else. Set the plan. Talk to your loved one about the necessary balance between adequate relief of discomfort and clarity of mind, and assure her you will be responsive to her wants and needs. Listen for indications of fear she may have of what will happen at the very end, and discuss with her how you will take care of these potential problems. Tell her you will see to it that she gets enough pain medication and that you will not allow her to suffer. Keep in mind that suffering is defined by the patient, not those observing her. Stay in contact with the doctor or nurse to ensure that your loved one will get the comfort care she needs.

Be with Her at the End

Dying patients may fear that their appearance or smells may bring loss of social support and alienation from their loved ones. And particularly they fear abandonment or dying alone. They want you with them at the end. If you live too far away to see your loved one frequently when she is dying, take responsibility to monitor her course well enough to get to her bedside with enough time to say your unhurried good-bye. This can be difficult. Many a family member has spent a week or weekend at a dying loved one's bedside, only to fly home not knowing the end would be two or three days later. If your own responsibilities make it impossible for you to return to your loved one's bedside within a day or two's notice, say good-bye when you leave after visiting her for a weekend. You don't have to say you might never see her again—just say all the rest of what goes into a final good-bye.

> **THE MOST important thing you can do for your loved one is to be sure she gets good comfort care.**

Help your loved one establish the memories she wants to leave with you. Go over those good times you had together and tell her the experiences with her you most enjoyed. Let her know you will always remember her fondly. Be open to her telling stories about you. Reminisce with her, and tell her you love her, and tell her you will think happily of her after she leaves.

Symptoms at the End

Be aware of the signs and symptoms of dying. Death is frequently not sudden but comes slowly over days. Loss of interest in eating and frequent and longer periods of sleep represent an involution of body and spirit. Do not see this as a turning away, but rather as a turning inward, a preparation for dying. Periods of seemingly senseless rambling or hallucination are common and represent a gradual release from normal mental functioning. There is no need to try to correct mistaken statements, or to point out that Aunt Lizzie, to whom your loved one is talking, has been dead for twenty years. Listen to your loved one's statements and reassure her about whatever she says. If she asks you to check on her mother—who died ten years ago—just say you will. These symptoms of slow deterioration are more common in prolonged, debilitating deaths, such as occur with cancer.

Helping Her Say Good-bye

Let her know that she will be in control of decisions until she is not able to make them anymore, at which time you will take care of her according to her wishes. Give her the assurance of your well-being, as that is likely to be a major concern of hers. Help her attend to unfinished business, of whatever nature and no matter how seemingly insignificant it may be. Don't tell her not to worry about it—tell her you'll take care of it. Help her attain spiritual readiness, in her way. Ask her forgiveness of your shortcomings, and allow her to ask the same of you.

If Suffering Worsens

If pain or discomfort worsens or becomes uncontrollable, you may have to help your loved one decide when to let go and broker more complete comfort care through the nurse or doctor. If pain relief is intermittent or inconsistent, with periods of unacceptable suffering, demand a means of more constant control. If your loved one is receiving intermittent dosing, as with pills, injections, or skin patches, ask for continuous intravenous infusion of whatever drug is necessary to accomplish smooth and continuous relief. Within days or hours of the end, decision making becomes almost impossible for a suffering or sedated patient, and you and other family members must assume this responsibility. If the time is appropriate and the situation requires it, you should signal to begin very aggressive comfort care or terminal sedation. Throughout it all, keep the lines of communication open with the medical providers.

Saying Good-bye

At the appropriate time, say good-bye and allow her to say good-bye to you. Do not fail in this, for your own sake as well as hers. She will leave, but you will live on with the knowledge of what you have said and not said. Tell her you and the family do not want to lose her, but you know it must happen and you do not dread it. Ask her forgiveness for your imperfections and outright transgressions, and forgive her if she asks to be forgiven. If you have unfinished business with her, finish it. Grieve for the loss of her love, not for your guilt about things left unsaid. Seek the reconciliation she wants and you will always need. Be there at the end. Hold her hand and say, "I love you."

Summary

1. Although serenity usually comes at the end, it is often short and follows a longer span of increased disability and physical symptoms.

2. If pain or suffering is severe or intractable, ask for enough aggressive comfort care to relieve your distress. If unacceptable symptoms return during cycles of consciousness, ask for continuous sedation.

3. Family members may have to help the dying person decide when to let go. Keep communication open with the medical providers, and be prepared to insist on more aggressive comfort care or terminal sedation.

4. Be sure to say good-bye.

APPENDIX I

Sample Living Will
and Durable Power of
Attorney Forms

FLORIDA LIVING WILL

Declaration made this _____ day of _____, 20____.

I, _____, willfully and voluntarily make known my desire that my dying not be artificially prolonged under the circumstances set forth below, and I do hereby declare:

If at any time I have a terminal condition and if my attending or treating physician and another consulting physician have determined that there is no medical probability of my recovery from such condition, I direct that life-prolonging procedures be withheld or withdrawn when the application of such procedures would serve only to prolong artificially the process of dying, and that I be permitted to die naturally with only the administration of medication or the performance of any medical procedure deemed necessary to provide me with comfort care or to alleviate pain.

It is my intention that this declaration be honored by my family and physician as the final expression of my legal right to refuse medical or surgical treatment and to accept the consequences for such refusal.

In the event that I have been determined to be unable to provide express and informed consent regarding the withholding, withdrawal, or continuation of life-prolonging procedures, I wish to designate, as my surrogate to carry out the provisions of this declaration:

Name: _____

Address: _____

_____ Zip Code: _____

Phone: _____

FLORIDA LIVING WILL — PAGE 2 OF 2

I wish to designate the following person as my alternate surrogate, to carry out the provisions of this declaration should my surrogate be unwilling or unable to act on my behalf:

PRINT NAME, HOME ADDRESS AND TELEPHONE NUMBER OF YOUR ALTERNATE SURROGATE

Name: _____

Address: _____

_____ Zip Code:_____

Phone: _____

ADD PERSONAL INSTRUCTIONS (IF ANY)

Additional instructions (optional):

I understand the full import of this declaration, and I am emotionally and mentally competent to make this declaration.

SIGN THE DOCUMENT

Signed: _____

WITNESSING PROCEDURE

Witness 1:
   Signed: _____
   Address: _____

TWO WITNESSES MUST SIGN AND PRINT THEIR ADDRESSES

Witness 2:
   Signed: _____
   Address: _____

Courtesy of **Choice In Dying, Inc.**　　6/96
1035 30th Street, NW Washington, DC 20007 800-989-9455

© 1996
CHOICE IN DYING, INC.

FLORIDA DESIGNATION OF HEALTH CARE SURROGATE

Name: _____
    (Last)   *(First)*   *(Middle Initial)*

In the event that I have been determined to be incapacitated to provide informed consent for medical treatment and surgical and diagnostic procedures, I wish to designate as my surrogate for health care decisions:

Name: _____

Address: _____

_____ Zip Code: _____

Phone: _____

If my surrogate is unwilling or unable to perform his duties, I wish to designate as my alternate surrogate:

Name: _____

Address: _____

_____ Zip Code: _____

Phone: _____

I fully understand that this designation will permit my designee to make health care decisions and to provide, withhold, or withdraw consent on my behalf; to apply for public benefits to defray the cost of health care; and to authorize my admission to or transfer from a health care facility.

Additional instructions (optional):

FLORIDA DESIGNATION OF HEALTH CARE SURROGATE — PAGE 2 OF 2

I further affirm that this designation is not being made as a condition of treatment or admission to a health care facility. I will notify and send a copy of this document to the following persons other than my surrogate, so they may know who my surrogate is:

PRINT THE NAMES AND ADDRESSES OF THOSE WHO YOU WANT TO KEEP COPIES OF THIS DOCUMENT

Name: _____

Address: _____

Name: _____

Address: _____

SIGN AND DATE THE DOCUMENT

Signed: _____

Date: _____

WITNESSING PROCEDURE

Witness 1:

Signed: _____

Address: _____

TWO WITNESSES MUST SIGN AND PRINT THEIR ADDRESSES

Witness 2:

Signed: _____

Address: _____

SAMPLE

Courtesy of **Choice In Dying, Inc.**   6/96
1035 30th Street, NW Washington, DC 20007 800-989-9455

© 1996
CHOICE IN DYING, INC.

APPENDIX 2

Organizations and Internet Sites

NOTE: this list is representative, not inclusive. For more Internet sites, search the web under the headings of: death and dying and hospice.

Organizations

National Cancer Institute (extensive information
    regarding cancer)
    Cancer Information Services
    P.O. Box 24128, Baltimore, MD 21227
    800-422-6237
    www.nci.nih.gov

Choice in Dying, Inc. (advance directives; links to most
    issues associated with dying)
    1035 30th St. N.W., Washington, D.C. 20007
    202-338-9790; 800-989-9455
    www.choices.org

The American Pain Foundation
    888-615-7246
    www.painfoundation.org

Compassion in Dying (right-to-die advocacy group)
    6312 SW Capital Hwy, Suite 415, Portland, OR 97201
    503-221-9556
    www.compassionindying.org

The Hemlock Society USA (right-to-die advocacy group)
    P.O. Box 101810, Denver, CO 80250
    800-247-7421
    www.hemlock.org

Hospice Foundation of America (comprehensive
    information about hospice)

2001 S. St. NW, Suite 300, Washington, D.C., 20009
202-638-5419
www.hospicefoundation.org

American Academy of Family Physicians (advance
      directives)
11400 Tomahawk Creek Parkway
Leawood, KS 66211
800-274-2237, ext. 5103
www.aafp.org

Funeral & Memorial Societies of America (information
      on range of funeral services)
P.O. Box 10, Hinesburg, VT 05461
800-765-0107
www.funerals.org/famsa

Compassionate Friends (bereavement support)
P.O. Box 3696, Oak Brook, IL 60522
630-990-0010
www.compassionatefriends.org

Advance Directives Web Sites

www.choices.org
      Web site of Choice in Dying. Advance directives.
      Links to most issues associated with dying.

www.aafp.org
      Advance directives and Do Not Resuscitate Orders

www.americangeriatrics.org
      Advance directives and Do Not Resuscitate Orders

Death and Dying Issues
Web Sites, General

www.growthhouse.org/links.html
Death and dying search engine and topic-specific
pages, with links to sites concerning hospice and
home care, palliative medicine, pain management,
quality improvement for end-of-life care, health care
directives, death with dignity, and bereavement.

www.choices.org/links.htm
A list of web sites dealing with death and dying
issues, with links to Web pages and organizations.

www.dyingwell.com
Web site of Dr. Ira Byock.

www.whitebuckpublishing.com.ale.aleqc.htm
Death and Dying—Christian links.

www.careofdying.org
Catholic healthcare organizations; supportive care of
the dying.

http:/www.globalideasbank.org/naturaldeath.html
List of books on dying.

Cancer; Pain Control Web Sites

cancer.mgh.harvard.edu/resources/ifgeneralsheets/dying.htm
Books and Web sites about cancer.

www.cancercare.org
Information on cancer.

cancernet.nci.nih.gov/index/html
National Cancer Institute web site.

www.lastacts.org
Palliative care and caring for dying patients.

Hospice Web Sites

www.aahpm.org
American College of Hospice & Palliative Medicine Web page.

www.agenet.com/hospice_links.html
Links to hospice and bereavement.

www.hospice-cares.com
Hospice information.

www.hospiceweb.com
Information about hospice, with links.

www.nho.org
National Hospice and Palliative Care Organization Web site.

www.virtualtrials.com/btlinks/hospice.cfm
Hospice care and related links.

Grief, Bereavement, Caregiving Web Sites

www.death-dying.org
Death and dying grief support.

www.opn.com/willowgreen
Willowgreen Web site: grief, illness, transition, caregiving.

www.rivendell.org
Grief net; death and dying resources.

www.compassionatefriends.org
Bereavement support.

SUGGESTED READINGS

Books

Albom, Mitch. *Tuesdays with Morrie*. New York: Double-day, 1997.

Best-selling inspirational book written by a journalist about his visits to a former teacher, who is slowly dying.

Battin, Margaret, ed. *Physician Assisted Suicide: Expanding the Debate*. New York: Routledge, 1998.

Essays by philosophers, ethicists, physicians, and lawyers on the leading-edge issues surrounding physician-assisted suicide.

Byock, Ira. *Dying Well*. New York: Riverhead Books, 1997.

Written by a noted hospice medical director, this book touches on nearly all the issues of dying through a series of case reports. Contains good, accurate de-scriptions of the medical problems of dying patients.

Callahan, Daniel. *The Troubled Dream of Life: Living with Mortality*. New York: Simon and Schuster, 1993.

A thoughtful book, written by a medical ethicist, about the social, ethical, and political issues our society faces in dealing with dying.

Dworkin, Gerald, R.G. Frey, and Sissela Bok. *Euthanasia and Physician-Assisted Suicide*. Cambridge, U.K.: Cambridge University Press, 1998.

Presents a pro and con debate of the philosophical, ethical, religious, and legal issues of physician-assisted suicide and euthanasia. Excellent reading for those who want to delve into the issues.

Fulghum, Robert. *All I Really Need to Know I Learned in Kindergarten: Uncommon Thoughts on Common Things.* New York: Mass Market Paperback, 1993.

Best seller by a philosopher/minister, who gives down- to-earth insights into the questions of dying through pithy and often amusing stories of everyday people. The chapter on "getting found" is particularly apropos for patients and their families.

Furman, Joan, and David McNabb. *The Dying Time.* New York: Bell Tower, 1997.

Written by a holistic nurse practitioner and a writer/ lawyer. Discussions include providing and caregiving for dying patients. An emphasis on psychological well-being, spirituality, and grieving.

Humphrey, Derek. *Final Exit.* Secaucus, N.J.: Carol Publishing, 1991.

A guide to self-deliverance. Practical, detailed advice on ending one's life.

Institute of Medicine. *Approaching Death.* Washington, D.C.: National Academy Press, 1997.

A scholarly treatise written for medical professionals. Full of statistics and information about all aspects of dying.

Jamison, Stephen. *Final Acts of Love.* New York: G.P. Putman's Sons, 1996.

Approvingly addresses assisted dying in detail and with great compassion. Particularly good for families and friends of patients who are considering assisted dying.

Lynn, Joanne, and Joan Harrold. *Handbook for Mortals: Guidance for People Facing Serious Illness.* New York: Oxford University Press, 1999.

Contains extensive and comprehensive medically-oriented information on preparing for dying, medical decision-making, pain and symptom control, forgoing medical treatment, and coping with events near death. Written by physicians. Reasoned arguments against physician-assisted suicide or hastening death.

Lattanzi-Licht, Marcia, John J. Mahoney, and Galen Miller. *The Hospice Choice: In Pursuit of a Peaceful Death*. Fireside, 1998.
The National Hospice Organization guide to hospice care. Everything you want or need to know about hospices.

McKhann, Charles. *A Time to Die*. New Haven, CT: Yale University Press, 1999.
The author, a surgeon at Yale, gives the definitive argument for assisted dying. This is probably the most comprehensive book on the subject written by a physician.

Nathan, Joel. *What to Do When They Say "It's Cancer": A Survivor's Manual*. St. Leonards, Australia: Allen & Unwin, 1998.
A practical guide, written by a cancer survivor, for people facing cancer. Especially helpful in coping psychologically. Lots of practical advice, all from the perspective of a patient.

Nuland, Sherwin. *How We Die*. New York: Knopf, 1994.
Best-selling book that is also excellent prose. A wise physician uses his experience with dying patients to give medical and ethical insight into the issues of dying.

Pearson, Cynthia, and Margaret L. Stubbs. *Parting Company: Understanding the Loss of a Loved One—The Caregiver's Journey*. Seattle: Seal Press, 1999.
Guidance for family caregivers in the home setting—

written by "lay" caregivers. If you are considering being a caregiver in the home, this book may be of great help.

Quill, Timothy. *Death and Dignity*. New York: W.W. Norton, 1993.

Fascinating ruminations about death and dying. This is not a source-book for patients but is particular-ly useful for understanding the dilemmas of physicians.

————. *A Midwife through the Dying Process*. Baltimore: The Johns Hopkins University Press, 1996.

The subtitle, Stories of Healing and Hard Choices at the End of Life, describes this excellent book, which discusses all the difficult choices dying patients face.

Ray, Catherine. *I'm With You Now*. New York: Bantam, 1997.

Written by a hospice educator, this excellent book is particularly strong in addressing the emotional and non-medical needs of patients, families, and friends.

Sankar, Andrea. *Dying at Home: A Family Guide for Caregiving*. New York: Bantam Books, 1995.

Advice for patients about what it's like to die at home with hospice care.

Schneiderman, Lawrence, and Nancy Jecker. *Wrong Medicine*. Baltimore: The Johns Hopkins University Press, 1995.

Important book about the many facets of futile therapy for dying patients, with chapters on "the way it ought to be" aimed at patients and physicians.

Shavelson, Lonny. *A Chosen Death*. New York: Simon & Schuster, 1995.

The author, a photojournalist and emergency-room physician, uses moving stories of patients to explain and support assisted dying.

Tobin, Daniel. *Peaceful Dying. The Step-by-Step Guide to Preserving Your Dignity, Your Choice, and Your In-ner Peace at the End of Life.* Reading, Mass: Perseus Books, 1999.

A guide to the process of dying, dealing with medical choices, and how to attain inner peace at the end of life.

Webb, Marilyn. *The Good Death.* New York: Bantam, 1997.

Probably the most sweeping advocacy of assisted suicide, placing the subject in the perspective of history, the law, and the age-old attempt to relieve the suffering of the dying. Not a practical guide to medical choices, but in it's breadth of discussion it touches all the important human considerations in dying.

Weenolsen, Patricia. *The Art of Dying.* New York: St. Martin's Griffin, 1996.

Practical and easy-to-read advice from a psychologist, who discusses physical, emotional and spiritual concerns of persons facing death.

National Cancer Institute Pamphlets

NOTE: National Cancer Institute publications are available by phone (800-4-CANCER) or on the Internet (http://www.nci.nih.gov).

Advanced Cancer. Living Each Day. National Cancer Institute, 1998. NIH Publication No. 98-856.

Eating Hints for Cancer Patients. Before, During & After Treatment. National Cancer Institute, 1998. NIH Publication No. 98-2079.

Get Relief from Cancer Pain. National Cancer Institute, 1994. NIH Publication No. 94-3735.

Helping Yourself During Chemotherapy. 4 Steps for Patients. National Cancer Institute, 1994. NIH Publication No. 94-3701.

Managing Cancer Pain. Patient Guide. AHCPR Publi-cation No. 94-0595, March, 1994.

Questions and Answers About Pain Control. A Guide for People with Cancer and Their Families. National Cancer Institute, 1995. NIH Publication No. 95-3264.

Radiation Therapy and You. A Guide to Self-Help During Treatment. National Cancer Institute, 1997. NIH Publication No. 97-2227.

Taking Time. Support for People with Cancer and the People Who Care About Them. National Cancer Institute, 1997. NIH Publication No. 98-2059.

Talking with Your Child About Cancer. National Cancer Institute, 1994. NIH Publication No. 94-2761.

When Cancer Recurs. Meeting the Challenge. National Cancer Institute, 1997. NIH Publication No. 97-2709.

Young People with Cancer. A Handbook for Parents. National Cancer Institute, 1993. NIH Publication No. 93-2378.

INDEX